M000040179

THE BELIEF ECONOMY

THE

HOW TO GIVE A DAMN,

BELIEF

STOP SELLING,

ECONOMY

AND CREATE BUY-IN

David Baldwin

LIONCREST
PUBLISHING

COPYRIGHT © 2017 DAVID BALDWIN
All rights reserved.

THE BELIEF ECONOMY
How to Give a Damn, Stop Selling, and Create Buy-In

ISBN   978-1-61961-803-9 *Hardcover*

978-1-61961-804-6 *Paperback*

978-1-61961-805-3 *Ebook*

FOR RENEE, CARY, AND NOLA.
YOU'RE THE REASON I GET
UP IN THE MORNING.

CONTENTS

FOREWORD

BY JOHN REPLOGLE

David Baldwin and I became neighbors for the first time, but certainly not the last, in 2006. Back then, I was president and CEO of Burt's Bees, and the company had just moved its offices to the American Tobacco Campus in Durham, North Carolina, a sprawling complex of historic buildings that once served as the United States' largest manufacturer of cigarettes but has since been sustainably redeveloped as a hub for entrepreneurs and mission-driven businesses.

We were welcomed into the community by McKinney, the advertising agency that occupied one of the neighboring offices, and its creative director, a friendly and cool cat named David Baldwin. As David and I came to know each other, I discovered his incredible talents as a creative advertising mind, innovator, entrepreneur, and even musician, but it was his passion for brands and his desire to see them have a positive impact on the world that struck me most. That mindset aligned with Burt's Bees' vision, so there was a lot of love shared between us neighbors.

Our friendship continued to grow through the mutual belief that business could be a powerful force for good, and that's why, when David left McKinney to start his own advertising agency, Burt's Bees became his first client. David and his team at Baldwin& wound up creating some award-winning work for us, including a campaign called "Find Your Burt." I loved that campaign; it cut right to the heart and soul of what Burt's Bees stands for. It reached the core of what we were, authentically shared our brand promise, and connected with the people who loved us. It was remarkable work and was recognized as such by critics.

As time passed, I was delighted to see Baldwin& grow to include more and more purpose-driven brands. Although my client-agency working relationship with David ended when I eventually left Burt's Bees to head up Seventh Generation, we continued to spark ideas and share values. Our values brought us together in many different forums, including the yearly B Corporation Champions Retreat, as well as the annual CEO Build for Habitat for Humanity, where we knocked nails together as we helped build houses across the Triangle.

When Seventh Generation wound up opening an office in Raleigh, who soon moved into the office right around the corner? David, of course. We were neighbors again in a different city. Our teams continue to share the same type of culture and values, and that again led to collaboration between us on a mission-driven personal care brand called Rooted Beauty.

I've loved reconnecting with David not only because he

and his team do fantastic work, but also because he truly understands and embraces the great global cultural awakening we are now experiencing. David, you the reader, and I—we are all connected. We are all one. This growing notion of the Belief Economy is occurring, in particular, within the younger folks in the millennial and Gen Z generations. It simply can't be ignored. The soap brand Dr. Bronner's, for instance, uses the slogan "We Are All One," and I think they're dead-on. In fact, Dr. Bronner's is one of those brands that just gets it; it sells soap absent of any synthetic or harmful ingredients, which is great, but it also embraces its beliefs of human goodness and unity.

Consumers are more connected today than ever before through digital devices and social media channels, but they're also more highly connected through their values. They are starting to understand that we can't simply keep taking from the planet without giving back. More than ever, consumers are looking beyond the label to discover how products are made, what the ingredients are, what goes into the packaging, and most importantly, what values and beliefs the company stands for. People are directing their purchases toward brands that truly reflect their values.

Brands must be clear about their purpose and what value they can add to people's lives. They must go beyond simply asking the questions, "What is the product I make, and why is it different?" Instead, brands must now ask, "Why does my company exist?" If you can't answer that question, you don't deserve to be in business today. It's the first question every CEO ought to ask, and frankly, it's a question that, when answered truthfully, authentically, and transparently, cuts to the heart of building brand trust. Successful businesses today must not only understand that but also embrace it. Purpose is the soul of all great brands.

In that vein, we have to completely rethink advertising and marketing. It's time to throw out the old playbook, which focused on painting a sleek veneer over your brand and widely amplifying that by buying access to consumers. The old model of advertising and marketing is dead. The new model is getting back to the heart and root of what your brand stands for, being crystal clear on your brand values, being authentic in your voice, and then approaching customers whom you have a relationship with in a much more intimate and social way, rather than through broad amplification. It's no longer about a sleek veneer. In fact, it's just the opposite; it's about humility, authenticity, and genuinely connecting with people.

It's a time of great optimism and success for brands that have embraced this fundamental shift in advertising and marketing, but also a time of concern for brands that haven't. Research has shown that 54 percent of Americans expect brands to be a force for positive change, and 57 percent say they will avoid brands they believe act unethically. As millennials and Gen Z continue to mature, these numbers will only increase.

We are all in this Belief Economy together, but David Baldwin understands the awakening that's upon us better than most. He's helped dozens of brands unearth their genuine values and beliefs, and have a positive impact by connecting with like-minded individuals through them. He will help you and your brand accomplish the same.

A BRIEF HISTORY OF THE FUTURE OF ADVERTISING.

Imagine, if you will, an interactive advertising campaign engaging in a two-way conversation via quirky language, compelling stories, and beautifully designed messages. Sometimes an ad in the campaign just asks the audience to check in with the brand to see if they have any thoughts to share.

The readers of this campaign liked it, so they shared their thoughts and their feelings and bought the products involved. Many kept in touch.

You'd probably say to yourself, "Uh, why are you describing just another Facebook campaign from any one of many different brands on my feed?" To which I'd counter, no, actually I'm describing one of many campaigns from the 1960s created by a fellow named Howard Luck Gossage, otherwise known as the "Socrates of San Francisco."

Howard's work was very different for the era—socially aware and active, sometimes politically interested, provocative, and not afraid to interact with customers in ways that had never been attempted. This magic happened mostly via print ads created with his partner, Margaret Larson, herself brilliant and trendsetting, and his little team of advernauts from the nascent times of the first creative revolution.

As great as Howard Gossage was, I've always wondered if

he might have become THE advertising guy of the century if he'd just been located in New York City like many of his more famous counterparts.

Regardless, Gossage's philosophy of engagement and selling has no better time and place than today with our plethora of tools and technology that allow you to actually pull off the shenanigans he was up to in simple print.

In his book *Changing the World Is the Only Fit Work for a Grown Man*, Steve Harrison, himself a brilliant copywriter, tells many of the behind-the-scenes stories and adventures of Gossage's all-too-short reign in the advertising business. (Gossage died relatively young at the age of fifty-two from cancer in 1969.)

Gossage wasn't just a fantastic copywriter; he was also a deep thinker on the subject of advertising and a philosopher on the impact of the business itself. Or as he once said, "Our first duty is not to the old sales curve, it is to the audience."[1]

More than any other time since, I believe we've fully entered the age of Gossage. Or, at least, we have the potential to if we play our cards right. We might just finish what Gossage started.

"Is advertising worth saving?" asked Gossage in an essay

about industry payment practices. "Yes, if we can learn to look at advertising not as a means for filling so much space and time but as a technique for solving problems."[2]

Well, fifty years ago, Gossage asked the essential premise of this entire Belief Economy endeavor.

Amen, brother.

To quote a study by Edelman: "From the grocery aisle to the car dealership, they're [consumers] buying on belief. Willing or not, brands of all kinds and sizes are now navigating this new reality. And in a lightning-digital world, the rewards and risks are equally high."

This may seem counterintuitive, but companies have an opportunity to adapt along with these new expectations.

Many of our greatest adherents say only selling matters in this business. Well, the traditional art of persuasion can lead to wonderful advertising, but like Gossage, I have to ask, is there something more we should be thinking about these days?

Maybe the question isn't whether we should sell. The question is, "Can we do more at the same time, and will it work?"

The Evolution of Advertising

Advertising is hardly a profound breakthrough of modern times. In fact, some of the earliest recorded ads can be dated back to Ancient Rome—those chariots weren't going to sell themselves. Whether it was chiseled in stone by the Romans, written on papyrus by the Egyptians, or announced in the streets by Europeans during the Middle Ages, advertisement has long been an essential tool for those selling their wares.

What *has* evolved dramatically about advertising in the last century is its level of sophistication, specifically in the research and study of human behavior. Birthed during the Great Depression era and nurtured across the idyllic suburban landscape of post-World War II America was the notion of consumption as a fundamental American value. Owning a home. Raising a family. Driving a new car every year. Buying lots of stuff. Keeping up with those damned Joneses. That was the American dream checklist. People weren't people anymore; they were now consumers, and they were encouraged by society to uphold those core beliefs.

If you study advertising from the 1940s and '50s, it doesn't take long to notice how illustrative of the times it is. It's full of sloganeering, bold proclamations, and of course, sexism. From that era emerged David Ogilvy, Bill Bernbach, and another advertising pioneer, Rosser Reeves, who made his name in television and was a proponent of the unique selling proposition.

These giants were driven by one goal above all others: To sell at all costs. Sell, sell, and sell some more. They cultivated their own set of principles and guidelines for accomplishing that goal, and their principles were widely adopted across the advertising world. Many of them were timeless: others, such as not dropping headline type out of photos, not so much.

Many times in my career have I heard the words, "I don't care if it's good work; I just want it to sell my product." Or to put it a better way, as overheard years ago, "That creative stuff is great and all, but I gotta move Funyuns." Well, of course, I agree. Let's move some Funyuns. But is there a new question that should be asked?

Is selling at all costs good enough anymore? Or can we sell even more with a new framework?

You Are Not a Consumer

You—yes, you—are not a consumer. You are a person, a son or daughter, husband or wife, boyfriend or girlfriend, father or mother. You are not simply a consumer of goods. Many brands understand this, but most do not.

The mere notion of consumption evokes images of locusts descending on a beautiful field of life-giving wheat and leaving it stripped bare. Of course, all living creatures must consume in order to survive, but consumption shouldn't define people in the marketplace. Human beings are far more complex than other creatures, even if we do tend to swarm malls and shopping centers and watch *The Big Bang Theory*. Our goals and concerns go deeper than mere survival. We are defined by our relationships, dreams, hopes, and aspirations.

So I'll say it again: We are not consumers. We are so much more, and savvy companies are finally waking up to that fact.

Is it time to challenge the notion that companies exist solely to sell their brand's products to consumers even though that's still job number one? Can a company stand for something and have a deeper impact on the world and, in doing so, sell more?

David Ogilvy himself said in *Confessions of an Advertising Man*, "The customer is not a moron. She's your wife."

That's what we'll be exploring.

The Game Has Changed

The times, as Bob Dylan famously sang, are a-changin', and they've brought a most welcome enlightenment. Don't get me wrong, I'm a capitalist through and through. I sell things for a living and have a deep respect for people who do the same, but there's no denying this simple truth: The scope of advertising has changed. There is an immense power in delivering messages to people through advertising, and with power comes a responsibility to wield it in a positive way.

We in the advertising and marketing business often think of ourselves as reflecting culture, but we create it as often as not, and we need to think about what it is we're creating.

Long before I founded the Baldwin& agency in 2009, I landed my first job in the advertising world at McCaffrey & McCall in New York. Ironically, David McCall, one of the agency's founders, had been Ogilvy's first copy chief. So as it turns out, I'm only two degrees separated from one of the masters.

At the time, 1985, Ogilvy's rule—sell at all costs—was still gospel, and my job provided a broad foundation in his advertising principles. After all, before you can break the rules, you have to understand them. Yet even then, I was driven by a compass that pointed toward more than just selling; I just didn't know how much more. I was selective about the products and clients I worked with (as much as possible for a youngster in the industry anyway). It was difficult to articulate in those days, but I knew there might be more to advertising than just selling.

Advertising used to feel like a simple scoring system: the more you sold, the more points you earned. Now, however, there may be a shift happening. Is it possible people—not consumers—want products to match their core values and beliefs?[3] Or at least not go against them? Is the game changing?

Whenever I hear people talk about the "end of advertising," I have to laugh. Advertising has literally never been more prevalent. Everywhere you turn, there's advertising; you can't get away from it. It's on television, radio, and billboards, and it has saturated the internet, which means it's all over your computer, cell phone, and tablet. Checking a social feed? There's an ad. Want to read an article on your favorite newspaper's website? Another ad. Watching a hilarious baby animal video on YouTube? Watch an ad first.

There's more advertising now than there's ever been in the history of humanity. Advertising isn't struggling. What is struggling are the old agency business models, and it's an important distinction to make.

Here's the best news of all: If you've read this far and thought, "Damn, I don't know what my brand's core values are, and I don't know what impact they can have beyond selling a product," take a deep breath and relax. The first step is to understand the need.

When I was a kid in El Paso, Texas, poking my way around the ad agency where my mother worked, I had no concept of the Belief Economy. I probably had no concept of the economy at all. But as I spent more time around the agency, I was drawn to the guys working on the creative side. I watched them, listened to them, and talked to them when I could. I did what human beings are inherently exceptional at: I learned. Even now, I still learn new things each and every day, whether it's how to use the latest technology, new slang, virtual reality headsets, or a new phone app.

You can learn how to position your company as a Belief-Driven Brand that connects and collaborates with people in our new values- and belief-oriented economy.

Generations and Brand Belief

Author Edward Abbey once wrote, "Growth for the sake of growth is the ideology of the cancer cell." He wasn't referring to advertising, but he may as well have been.

That one simple sentence has stuck with me for a long time. Growth for the sake of growth was certainly the mentality of the era. That type of advertising might have been effective for baby boomers (born between 1946 and 1964) and Gen Xers (1965–1979), but it is not as effective for millennials (1980–1995) and Gen Z (1996–2010), or as I prefer, iGen, a term coined by Center for Generational Kinetics CEO Denise Villa.

Millennials are not merely interested in a product but also in what the brand selling the product stands for and is contributing to the world. A brand's values and impact may be even more important to iGen, and research indicates both generations' purchasing decisions are influenced by that knowledge.[4] There is much, much more to explore as it pertains to the world's two youngest generations, but this much is abundantly clear: brands *must* have a clearly defined belief system and be aligned with it or possibly risk facing backlash.

While currently not the biggest spenders, millennials and iGen will form the most influential group of customers over the next half a century, so understanding how to market your brand to them is critical in the changing landscape of marketing and advertising.

This book will help you move in a new direction by exploring the traits and behaviors of millennials and iGen, the increasing importance of creating Shared Value with your customers, and examples of companies that have gotten it right and wrong. It will also help create an actionable plan specific to your brand through workshops and exercises designed to:

- Identify and articulate your brand's core beliefs and values
- Create collaboration with your customers through those values
- Keep your brand ahead of the curve in a rapidly changing landscape
- Help you to have a positive impact on the world

Every brand has its own unique path to becoming truly Belief-Driven. The trick, of course, is successfully locating and navigating that path.

A NEW KIND OF CONSUMPTION AND WHY IT MIGHT CONSUME YOU.

The Belief Economy: The combined economic buying power and influence of the millennial and iGen generations.

Raise your hand if you remember the DEX machine. Anyone? Bueller? Well, long before Facebook, Instagram, and Snapchat were ingrained in the fabric of our society, there was a wonderful piece of equipment that could magically send documents across the country in mere minutes. OK, half hours, but still.

If you're thinking to yourself, "That sounds like a fax machine," that's because it was. But back in 1985, the fax machine was the hottest, most revolutionary piece of technology anyone had seen in our business. I was just a dopey, fresh-faced kid right out of college, but the veterans around the office were floored. "You're not going to believe this," they said. "I can take a script, send it through this machine, and in twenty minutes, it'll be waiting for the creative director in Los Angeles." How far we've come. Now with the click of a mouse, or the swipe of a thumb, you can chat face-to-face with a friend or coworker across the world instantaneously.

In the 1990s, cell phones and laptops took over as the internet exploded. In the 2000s, the rise of social media began with websites like Myspace and Facebook. In the

2010s, the second social media wave arrived with Instagram and Snapchat. Who knows what the 2020s hold in store? Writer and professor of media studies Clay Shirky said it best: "Technology is truly not revolutionary until it's boring."

The emergence of the internet and social media is not the sole reason the Belief Economy now exists, but it is one element of a more complicated formula. Millennials and iGen are impact-minded groups. They want to have a positive impact on the world, and they expect the brands they invest in to share the mission. What the internet and social media have fostered is a greater sense of connectedness and community. It's easier than ever to learn what brands stand for and to connect with other people who share similar beliefs.

The technological outlets for expressing these beliefs are specific to our current era, but if you study history, you'll notice patterns often repeat themselves. The world's two youngest generations share much in common with generations from the last century.

Generational Patterns of Repetition

At face value, you might think millennials have little in common with the World War II (WWII) generation.

There's a gap of roughly eighty years, which spans multiple periods of war, economic strife, and technological advances. The WWII generation, sometimes referred to as the Greatest Generation, includes people born between roughly 1900 and 1925. Think about what that generation faced, including the Great Depression and a world war, yet they emerged to create the greatest prosperity the world has ever seen. The WWII generation essentially built the modern infrastructure of America.

External factors such as the rise of cell phones and the internet are superficial. On a deeper level, generations actually exhibit similar traits that are repeated in sequential order. This phenomenon is explored on an unparalleled level in the book *Generations: The History of America's Future, 1584 to 2069*, by William Strauss and Neil Howe. The two detail their theory, along with significant supporting evidence, that every generation has one of four sets of specific traits, and these traits repeat themselves in a pattern.

Four generational events, referred to as "turnings" by Strauss and Howe, follow a specific pattern: High, Awakening, Unraveling, Crisis. This is the four-stage cycle of social moods, with each stage spanning roughly twenty years:

- **High:** Institutions are strong, but individualism is

weak. Society as a whole is confident. Occurs after a Crisis.

- **Awakening:** Institutions decline as individualism grows. Occurs after a High.
- **Unraveling:** Institutions are weak, but individualism is strong. Occurs after an Awakening.
- **Crisis:** Institutional life is destroyed, typically due to a war or other destructive event. Occurs after Unraveling.

Additionally, there are four cyclical generation archetypes that coincide with these turnings and describe the people who constitute different generations:

- **Prophet:** Driven by morals and principles. Born near the end of a Crisis.
- **Nomad:** Often alienated but practical leaders. Born during an Awakening.
- **Hero:** Energetic, often overconfident as adults. Born during an Unraveling.
- **Artist:** Overprotected but grow into leaders. Born during a Crisis.

Despite being released in 1991, three years before the demarcation line between millennials (hero) and iGen (artist), Strauss and Howe predicted exactly what's happening in our society right now.

They predicted baby boomers would go to their graves pissed off, hissing at one another and fighting to their last breaths, which has held true. Look no further than the current state of our opinion- and outrage-based news landscape via cable and radio networks. The standard operating procedure for these broadcasts is to put two opposing views across a table from each other and let them duke it out, often viciously, until a "winner" is left standing. Perhaps the most incredible of all was the correct prediction of the collapse of institutions. All you need to do is look around you. Strauss and Howe predicted institutions across the country would collapse; they have before and they will again. The generational pendulum has swung back to that point—what you're seeing right now is an undoing of the Great Society that was formed in the 1960s. An Unraveling right into a Crisis.

> **"Generations tend to raise their kids not as mirror images...but as complements of themselves."**

At the time of this writing, the current governmental structures are doing everything they can to dismantle all of the traditional standards of the United States administrative state, or "drain the swamp," as they call it. According to Strauss and Howe, right on time and, in fact, inevitable.

Well, once these institutions crumble, who will rebuild the

world? Millennials, of course, with a healthy dose of iGen ingenuity to boot. It happened with the Greatest Generation and the Silent Generation (1925-1942) following World War II. The world was decimated. Everything had to be reinvented and rebuilt, and from those ashes came a rise in nationalism. We don't yet know the full extent of the current rise in nationalism, but you can see it happening across the globe, including here in the United States.

As Howe sees it, "Generations tend to raise their kids not as mirror images...but as complements of themselves." That's perhaps an oversimplified way of looking at it, but sometimes the truth is simple. Generations are influenced by the previous generation, both positively and negatively. Typically, a generation will attempt to solve the perceived mistakes of the previous generation, which explains why the children of hippies didn't also become hippies—they became capitalists. The world went from peace, free love, and the Age of Aquarius to the bitter cynicism of Gen Xers, who vowed to be everything their divorced parents weren't. All of which has now led us to the pattern of inflated self-esteem we find in millennials, who are damned with the notion of receiving trophies for doing no more than participating.

These generational patterns are certainly a fascinating exploration of people and the specific generational traits that rise and fall in humanity, but beyond that, they are keys to crucial information for marketers. What's on the way? Can we predict macrotrends? For instance, if the generational patterns hold, we're a generation away from another spiritual awakening. There was one in the 1960s with the baby boomers, so the pattern will repeat.

All of this is important because it helps us understand not just the current generations' thinking and makeup but also the context for their behavior and how they might behave in the marketplace now and in the future.

Replace Consumption with Collaboration?

The rise of baby boomers in the mid-1900s also coincided with the outcome and increase of "consumption" and "consumerism" as standard American ideas and values. "Consumer" has been used in the seventy years since to describe any person who buys a good or service. Maybe it's time to update our advertising vocabulary.

If you couldn't already tell, the word *consumer* irks me. I admit this understanding of consumers as individual people only fully formed for me when I had children. From the moment I held them in my arms to their college searches and beyond, they will always be my children: human beings I hope are going to be productive individuals and add to society in a positive way. My wife and I are not the parents of consumers; we are parents of people.

Think about it this way: To whom are you actually selling? It's not some nameless, faceless entity known as the consumer. It's brothers and sisters, kids and parents, neighbors and friends. If you were selling something to a close friend's daughter, for instance, how would your behavior change? You wouldn't be trying to sell, sell, sell at all costs anymore.

> **What if we instead viewed the people we're selling to as participants or collaborators?**

What if we instead viewed the people we're selling to as participants or collaborators? What if we collaborated *with* them to help them figure out what to buy and how to buy it, while simultaneously having a positive impact on their lives?

The word *consumer* dehumanizes people, reducing them to faceless numbers who exist solely to spend. The notion could not be further from the objective behind creative advertising, marketing, and messaging. The goal is to create things to motivate, delight, and inspire people. You should genuinely want to make them happy, make them laugh, and make them engaged, not just make them "consume."

This isn't a change that will happen overnight. The term *consumer* is so deeply embedded in the advertising and marketing industries, and culture itself, that it couldn't possibly be eradicated quickly. But maybe the seeds just need to be planted.

The idea of consumerism changed the trajectory of capitalism. Consumption was not always an American value, but we've adopted it as such. Doing the right thing, helping your neighbor, freedom—those were American values. We've since added "buying things" to that list, and the idea of consumerism is one of the reasons why.

Consumption doesn't merely apply to items you buy in a store or online but also to the websites, apps, and other technologies you "consume." The harsh reality is that a chunk of our economy is built around small moments of joy that can have a negative impact that lasts thousands of years. Think about those silly little chattering teeth people buy each other as a gag. They're cheap novelty items, yet they are made of plastic, and resources from a factory somewhere in the world were required to create them. Packaging was created to house them. Oil and gas were needed to distribute them. As a gift, maybe the silly teeth merit about thirty seconds of laughter, followed by one month of sitting among desk clutter, only to be tossed in the trash and taken to a landfill. That is the very definition of what writer George Monbiot calls "pathological consumption."[5]

The paradigm shift in favor of consuming dates back to the twentieth century, and it was in very good hands. A number of the founding mothers and fathers of selling impacted the industry in their own ways. Bill Bernbach, of the seminal creative agency Doyle Dane Bernbach, was a major influence in advertising's creative revolution through today. Mary Wells brought a visceral experiential truth to her work. And as stated previously, Howard Luck Gossage was a brilliant innovator in creating dialogue with his audience through his copywriting and inclusion of coupons in advertisements.

These giants were writing new rules as they went and were a bastion for selling in a more human fashion. They produced brilliant, emotionally resonant, persuasive advertising, but all toward a very specific goal: sell, sell, sell. In their era, people were, for the most part, consumers, beings to be persuaded into buying products.

The Belief Economy in Action

Millennials and iGen seem to be impact-driven generations.[6] They aren't asking for brands to take a stand; together, in a soup of current mores and older generations, they're often demanding it. You might not realize it, but you've already been exposed to the idea of the Belief Economy. We see examples, both positive and negative, on a seemingly daily basis. Something happens at odds with a specific belief system, and the market responds.

Here are just a few:

Chobani

Hamdi Ulukaya, the Turkish founder of Chobani yogurt, decided to play his part in the refugee crisis by hiring them to work in his yogurt manufacturing plants. These were refugees, representing nineteen different nationalities, who had been resettled by the US government. He even helped them physically get to the plant, and he put translators on the manufacturing floor to help make it all work. Ulukaya's actions drew extreme reactions from many sides of our culture, but he felt it was important to live his values.[7] While the reaction was heated, Chobani has now overtaken Yoplait in the marketplace and is posting double-digit sales.[8] This is certainly not because he hired refugees, but he always leads with his values.

Speaking of Refugees, Starbucks

Starbucks doesn't just sell delicious coffee. Their values

are baked into their business model and guide them as a brand. So, in 2017, when then CEO Howard Schultz announced that in response to President Trump's immigration ban Starbucks would be hiring ten thousand refugees across its stores worldwide, it wasn't just a marketing gimmick.

Starbucks believes in supporting immigrants. The first value it lists on its website is, "Creating a culture of warmth and belonging, where everyone is welcome." That sounds great, of course, but it doesn't mean much if you aren't walking the walk. Pledging to aid ten thousand refugees at a time when there is considerable debate and strife surrounding immigrants worldwide is simply staying true to the company's values.

The pledge elicited reactions from both sides—devotees of the brand who strongly supported Starbucks, and Trump supporters who called for a boycott—but it aligned with the company's and the customers' beliefs and values. They took a stand.

Chick-fil-A

A similar situation arose with Chick-fil-A back in 2012, following negative comments about same-sex marriage made by the company's CEO. This drew strong, passionate reactions from those for and against same-sex marriage.

There were protests and boycotts of the fast food chain, but interestingly enough, this was countered by a Belief Economy that supported Chick-fil-A in record numbers.

It's not for me to sort out who's right and who's wrong, but it's further proof we've moved into an era of people choosing to act on their beliefs and vote with their wallets.

Ivanka Trump's Clothing Lines

In February 2017, Nordstrom and Neiman Marcus stopped selling Ivanka Trump-branded clothing. It wasn't an altogether shocking move, given the divisiveness surrounding the Trump name, but the results since the decision have been surprising.

Rather than fade into obscurity, sales of Ivanka's clothing lines skyrocketed in the following weeks. Why is that? Because people vote with their values and their wallets, and they apply these values to the decisions they make in the free market.

The concept of slacktivism, or supporting a political or social cause via action on the internet, is often spoken of negatively, but I see it as a positive. Presidential elections come around once every four years, but the reality is, we get to vote every day. Every time slacktivists take out their wallets to buy something online, they get to cast a vote.

We've used fairly prickly political issues in these examples, so does this mean the answer is to use your political beliefs to sell your products? Wading into politics isn't for the faint of heart, and I don't recommend it unless it is central to your company's ethos or mission. If your company is fundamentally oriented around whatever issue you're taking a stand on, then by all means. Otherwise, it can be tough sledding.

The point is, more than ever, purchases can be statements of values and beliefs.[9]

Defining Your Brand

How are you using your belief system to create what you do, to manufacture what you do, and to sell what you do? This goes deeper than a marketing campaign to boost sales. "Greed is good," a saying popularized by *Wall Street*'s Gordon Gekko, truly was the slogan for the 1980s. What started as a social commentary on how bad greed is turned into a rallying cry: prestige and selling, selling and prestige. People weren't engaged in the same way they are now.

Great brands have always come from a genuine belief system. "Just Do It" is not simply a nifty marketing slogan Nike stumbled upon. I don't have access to any of Nike's internal marketing documents, but I'd be willing to bet their belief system is built around the concept that anyone can compete and there's an athlete in all of us. Just look at their work over the last thirty-five years. That exact ethos shines through in everything they do, whether it's creating a tiny phone-connected device that fits inside your shoe or creating shoes and clothes to fuel competition. It's not an advertising proposition; it's the way the company operates. The advertising is merely an extension of the belief, not BS sloganeering. Do they have issues with how their products are made overseas? You bet they do, and because of this dissonance with their stand, people got mad at them. So they tackled these issues in a powerful chain of events and partnerships to address and support positive change. They had to.

Voilà! The Belief Economy in action.

Companies have always had mission statements. The problem was, the company mission statement didn't always align with the separate marketing mission, which would typically be centered on getting results at any cost. When you're a public company being judged on quarterly earnings, you're in a most unfortunate position. How can you set and achieve long-term goals if you're constantly sacrificing the vision for short-term gains to satisfy shareholders? The short answer of course is, you can't always do it. Quarterly thinking can be toxic.

The question then becomes this: Why wouldn't you try to reach all these engaged customers who are making decisions with their wallet? Your job as a marketer is to engage someone with your story and beliefs and convince them to buy your product. Too many clients get confused by values-driven advertising and say, "This is too much. I just need to sell my stuff. Sell, sell, sell." But remember, you're not trying to sell your product once or twice.

The difference now, of course, is the stakes are high. You *need* to have your belief system clearly defined. Companies that don't are going to be left behind, because engaged people are paying attention.

You Have to Give a Damn

The Baldwin& internal agency mantra is simple but powerful: Give a damn about everything you do. We constantly talk about this internally with our employees and externally with the clients we work with. Give a damn about what's in front of you, the job you're working on, your families, and the impact your work will have on the culture.

Baldwin& is a B Corp, which is to business what Fair Trade is to coffee. B Corps are companies that use their business influence to make a positive impact on the world. Most B Corps are manufacturers, as they can demonstrably prove what they make and the impact it has, but our agency was also able to attain B Corp status for a few reasons: the way we treat our employees, the way we operate, and the frequency with which we give back.

We provide insurance coverage of 100 percent for all of our employees. Are there cheaper alternatives that would save the company money? Of course. But cutting corners to save cash at the expense of our employees' health and well-being would fly directly in the face of everything we stand for.

Our entire philosophy revolves around the notion of giving a damn, and our mission as an agency is to use our creativity for clients whom *we* believe in.

I share this not to brag about Baldwin& but simply to illustrate how giving a damn can permeate a company. We have a strong belief system that defines who we are, and we operate from this set of values in everything we do. It's important to us to demonstrate to clients in a genuine way what we're all about.

Decisions are made emotionally. Sure, some people base their shopping solely on price. That will always be part of the equation, and in fact, millennials in particular are often saddled with student debt, so their finances are an issue.

> "If people only made rational decisions, they'd only shop at the Dollar Store."

But if people only made rational decisions, they'd only shop at the Dollar Store. The majority of people make decisions based on emotion and then justify rationally, so you want the emotion elicited by your brand to be a positive one. By proving you give a damn, you'll earn an authentic emotional response that can actually render the price *a* consideration and not *the* consideration.

Lean into Fear

Change is scary. That's true in all walks of life. Human beings are creatures of habit, and facing the unknown often means breaking those habits. In advertising, the tried-and-true ways of marketing have existed for decades, and it feels safe to stick with what you know. And it's important to note, we're not talking about losing the fundamentals of marketing; we're talking about the potential to layer a new set of meaning onto what you're already doing.

Don't resist the change—lean into it. On the other side of fear is opportunity, and that's something we preach at Baldwin&. Sacrifice is the essence of opportunity. A company's message should be direct and focused, not wide and unfocused. There is tremendous power in a simple thought. No one understands this more than the agency Ogilvy. For instance, the Dove Campaign for Real Beauty promotes the idea that everyone, no matter their shape, size, age, or race, is beautiful. It's a simple thought that had a profound impact and opened up a world of opportunities for Dove and, not to mention, a growth in sales from 2.5 billion to 4 billion since the campaign's inception.[10]

Many companies are started for a reason other than to solely make money. At the very beginning, there was at least one person who simply had a passion for something. Over time, that passion may have become buried under jargon and other corporate nonsense, causing a company to lose its guiding light. It's still there, though, ready to be unearthed and brought back into focus.

Purpose, impact, and emotion—those are the areas brands must also focus on. Why do you do what you do, and why do you care about it? What kind of *impact* can your brand have beyond the advertising and sale of a product? What emotion do you stand for? All of these questions require careful consideration. Don't run from this. You can't afford to anymore. It's time to lean in and give a damn.

CHAPTER 1 HIGHLIGHTS

A quick look back at the most salient takeaways from chapter 1:

- **Generational patterns:** History has a way of repeating itself, particularly when it comes to generations. Technological advances such as cell phones and the internet are superficial. On a deeper level, generations exhibit similar traits that are repeated in sequential order.

- **Consumption? Try collaboration:** The term *consumer* dehumanizes people, reducing them to faceless entities that represent nothing more than dollar signs. Brands in the Belief Economy must not just sell to consumers; they must also motivate and inspire people to be in it with them.

- **Purpose, not just products:** The Belief Economy demands that brands have a clearly defined purpose and authentic belief system. Brands without those may be left behind as the economic buying power and influence of millennials and iGen continues to grow.

MILLENNIALS AND GEN Z: MAYBE THEY DESERVE A TROPHY AFTER ALL.

There are no perfect definitions of millennials and Gen Z, or iGen, as I'll continue to refer to them (hat tip again to Denise Villa). Generational designations are, at best, imperfect, but they exist to create identifiable groups—cohorts, in our parlance. If you were born between 1980 and 1995, you're generally considered a millennial, and if you were born between 1996 and 2010, you're considered part of the iGen. There are significant shades of gray, of course. A person born in 1980 is thirty-seven years old in 2017, while someone born in 1995 is only twenty-two years old. Those are two completely different life stages, yet, technically, both individuals are millennials. So segmentations into any generation are an absolute must, to say the least.

An odd but true fact about advertisers is that they tend to focus on younger demographics. Baby boomers aren't completely ignored, nor should they be, because for now they're the biggest spending generation. In fact, baby boomers spend the most across all product categories but are targeted by just 5 percent to 10 percent of marketing dollars.[11] Their shopping habits are a bit different than those of millennials and iGen. Maybe that's why, for instance, you typically don't see older men driving new cars in commercials. A company like Cadillac will show a younger guy driving their car so the older, gray-haired guys will stop and say, "I want to be that guy." Everyone wants to be young again, right?

It's impossible to attribute a reliable figure to the economic weight millennials and iGen carry, but from the figures I've seen, iGen currently influences somewhere around $600 billion a year in family spending.[12] And it's estimated that millennial buying power and influence could grow to $1.4 *trillion* by 2020.[13] But who are millennials, really? What are iGen like as people? What makes these two youngest generations tick? We know this much: Millennials and iGen are drawn to brands and companies that possess an authentic passion, purpose, and/or ideology that align with their own.[14] It's easy to assume there have never been generations quite like these two, and while no two generations are ever completely identical, historical trends can shine a light on what's to come.

Follow the Patterns

As we highlighted in the previous chapter, William Strauss and Neil Howe put forth the theory that generational patterns repeat throughout history. If their predictions hold to form, there will be a complete restructuring of the rules and institutions over the next twenty years. Right now, cynical-minded Gen X controls all of the major institutions, but the impact-minded generations (millennials in particular) aren't far from taking over.

Remember, one of the hallmarks of Strauss and Howe's

generational patterns is that children tend to be a complement of their parents' generation, rather than a carbon
copy. Parents generally don't raise kids who are exactly like
them but instead complement their perceived strengths
and weaknesses. Think of it this way: every generation is
directly impacted by the one preceding it. Let's connect
the dots for millennials and iGen.

If you think back to the 1960s and '70s, what was happening with the baby boomers? There was a profound
spiritual awakening. Hippies, flower power, peace, and
free love, baby. On closer inspection, however, it's not
hard to see what broke down the institution of marriage.
We're looking at you, free love. People got divorced in
droves and abortions skyrocketed in the '70s. The generation raised by baby boomers, Generation X, didn't adopt
the free-loving, carefree ways of their parents. Instead,
they grew up cynical, full of angst and uncertainty. The
hippie, feel-good music of their parents gave way to angry,
alternative rock and grunge. When Gen X began to have
kids of their own, the view of marriage had changed. They
didn't want to repeat the patterns of their parents, so they
stayed married longer[15] and showered their children with
the encouragement they never received.

What we've ended up with is an incredibly confident generation of millennials who believe they deserve great

things. They were given those dreaded participation trophies for tournaments they didn't win. They were told, "You can be anything you want," except as they've transitioned from college into the working world, they've found out it's a little bit harder than that. Millennials entered the workforce with an incredibly confident mindset that annoyed baby boomers and Gen X alike. The older generations are predictably guarded. "Wait a minute," they shout. "I had to work my butt off to get here, and they come in wanting as much money and thinking they deserve a senior-level job? No way."

How Millennials, iGen Differ

There was an illustrative article in the *New York Times* back in 2015 in which Lucie Green, the worldwide director of the innovation group at the J. Walter Thompson Company, compared millennials to the character of Hannah Horvath from the TV show *Girls*.[16] Lena Dunham's character is completely self-absorbed, but she's also constantly asking herself, "How can I have an impact? What's the right thing to do? How can I be the right person, right now?"

Green's iGen comparison was Alex Dunphy from *Modern Family*. If you've never seen the show, she's the younger daughter who's a studious high achiever, but she's also more of a nervous realist. She's actively involved in events surrounding her life, and she authentically tries to make a difference by doing the right thing. These are, of course, just two examples from two well-known TV shows. I'm not suggesting every millennial act like Hannah Horvath or every iGen act like Alex Dunphy, but some comparative perspective is always helpful.

Millennials are highly optimistic, more so than iGen, and there's a sobering reason. Millennials have been flooded with a constant wave of pampering and reassuring from parents, teachers, and other adults. *You can do anything. You can be anything.* And, of course, let's not forget about those much-maligned participation trophies. iGen, on the other hand, grew up with, or in the aftermath of, September 11, a day that changed the tenor of the American psyche going forward. This type of cataclysmic event has made iGen not only more guarded but also more pragmatic in their approach to life. iGen has undoubtedly been influenced by millennials and, in particular, their disappointments.

Millennials and iGen are definitively split on the concept of selling out. To millennials, it's a dirty word symbolizing the surrender of your values. To iGen, it's a smart business decision to capitalize on one's uniqueness. This concept is explored in the PBS documentary *Generation Like*, which highlights the growing number of YouTube and internet stars making a living for themselves by being...themselves.

> **Millennials and iGen are more motivated by the purpose and impact of their actions and the experiences they take part in than by the money they're making.**

The notion of selling out is something iGen embraces as a strong choice for personal brands. You need look no further than the Kardashians, a revered family among iGen. The reality TV movement has transformed the stars of those shows into brands. I remember Gene Simmons once saying KISS was a rock brand, not a rock band. That might have been many years ago, but the sentiment still rings true with contemporary musical artists, celebrities, and athletes.

Millennials Want a Mission to Fulfill Them; iGen Want to Fulfill a Mission

Keep in mind all of these descriptions and characteristics are generalizations. Not every iGen is an overachieving realist. Not every millennial is an entitled brat who demands a trophy simply for showing up. In fact, that particular stereotype is rooted in the tattooed-white-hipster mythology, while actually, nearly 45 percent of all millennials are minorities, making them the most racially diverse generation ever.[17]

So these generalizations will often blur the line between stereotypes. What people often misconstrue as millennials' entitlement is actually a deep desire to make a difference. When the desire is unfulfilled, there's a palpable disappointment older generations perceive as entitlement. And we have to be honest with ourselves that all of this might just be the zeitgeist of the age.

Simon Sinek, author of the best-selling leadership book, *Start with Why*, has written extensively about the golden circle. Picture a large circle with two smaller circles layered inside of it. The outside ring is a company's what, as in what they do. The middle ring is the how, as in how the company creates its what. And the smallest ring in the center is the why. Why does a company do what it does? What's the deeper purpose?

Millennials and iGen are more motivated by the purpose and impact of their actions and the experiences they take part in than by the money they're making.[18] Don't get me wrong, they want to make money and know they need to. But sometimes the first question they're asking isn't, "How much is the salary?" They want to know if what they're doing is important. iGen want to join companies with which they can have an immediate and tangible impact.[19] Millennials don't want to just head into an office every day, sit in a cubicle, and become a drone. "Put in five years and pay your dues. That's how it's always been" is not something a millennial wants to hear. Instead, why not take millennials and put them in charge of a facet of the company in which they *can* have an impact?

I have *never* looked at millennials as entitled or as a detriment. In fact, I utterly reject the notion that they're entitled brats. To me, it's amazing when they want to come in and make such an impact right away. If you were hiring a staff, wouldn't you want your employees to truly be interested in making a difference? Hire millennials. That's what we've done at Baldwin&, which mostly employs millennials, and they've been fantastic employees.

Millennials watched their parents work thirty years for the same employer before retiring with a token watch and a lifetime full of regret, and they'll be damned if they're going to repeat this path. Millennials are passionate, optimistic, and genuinely want to be a piece of a bigger picture. To me, this is the complete opposite of lazy and entitled. Don't resist millennials; embrace them.

CHAPTER 2 HIGHLIGHTS

A quick look back at the most salient takeaways from chapter 2:

- **Know your audience:** Millennials (born between 1980–1995) alone will account for well over $1 trillion by 2020. iGen may currently be influencing up to $600 billion in family spending.

- **What millennials want:** While self-interested, millennials are motivated to make a difference. They tend to seek careers in which they can make a real impact, and they expect the brands they support to take authentic stands.

- **Don't forget iGen:** Both generations are driven by the purpose and impact of their actions. But seeing millennials struggle has influenced iGen, making them more pragmatic.

CAPITALISM AS A FORCE FOR GOOD, PROVING ONCE AND FOR ALL, KARL MARX WAS A SCHMUCK.

Capitalism, in its simplest definition, is an economy in which private owners control their own businesses and production. In other words, it's a free market. Connected capitalism, sometimes referred to as "conscious capitalism" or "capitalism with a conscience," goes a bit deeper. Regardless of your preferred term, the idea is the same. It signifies the notion that everything in life is connected and you can have an impact with what you do. By embracing the idea of connected capitalism, you would create a business model built around making money *and* doing good.

Making money is great. Like I've said before, that's capitalism, baby. But millennials and iGen expect you and your company to stand for more than simply raking in dough. This doesn't mean you have to be leading the charge to save the world, but it does mean you need more than just a single bottom line of profit. How can you measure the impact of your brand on the world? Profit isn't enough. Connected capitalism requires a double bottom line: making profit and doing good. If doing good is too broad, you can consider a triple bottom line: profit, people, and planet.

This concept is in direct opposition to Gordon Gekko's aforementioned "Greed is good" speech. That, of course, was intended to be a satirical commentary on the day but instead was adopted as an ethos for the age. I was living in New York shortly after the movie was released, and it felt like everyone was quoting it. *Greed is good. Greed is good.* If you listen closely, you might even still hear

> **Connected capitalism requires a double bottom line: making profit and doing good.**

certain contemporary politicians echoing the phrase's sentiment. For the most part, however, this me-first attitude is declining in the wake of the Belief Economy's emergence.

Burt's Bees Gets It

When I founded Baldwin&, Burt's Bees was ranked number one on the list of companies I wanted to work with. To be honest, they were my number one years before Baldwin& became a reality, but as often is the case in the advertising world, it just never worked out. That finally changed in 2009 when, after a bit of luck and a fortuitous meeting set up by one of our employees, we landed a project with the company for Earth Day.

The resultant campaign was called "Find Your Burt." Burt's Bees founder, Burt Shavitz, lived off the grid in a converted turkey coop in Maine and served as the overarching inspiration. Our message to people was simple: You can make a difference in the world by making small differences, voting with your wallet, and making choices that matter to you. Sound familiar? We couldn't ask everyone to be quite as committed as Shavitz—turkeys usually have dibs on their coops anyway. But the idea was, everyone has a little bit of Burt inside of them, and that alone could make a difference.

Leading up to Earth Day, the campaign centered on creating an invitation to action and collaboration. A website created a fun journey through Burt's values and his story of attending the world's first Earth Day.

The site included the ability to learn your own level of "Burtness" using a simple survey about your lifestyle, and depending on your answers, you were awarded different levels of beardiness to transform yourself into various degrees of the hirsute founder, from mutton chops to full-on Burt Beard. Just how "Burt" are you? Your transformed photo became shareable content on relevant social channels.

Then, on Earth Day itself, organic Burt kits were handed out at events including a Burt beardana (custom bandanas that, when wrapped around a person's face, made it look like they had a Burt Beard), lip balm, and an organic cotton conductor's hat (one of Burt's trademark accessories). These sample kits were handed out by Burt lookalikes.

To prove just how natural the products really are, people could also use a pedal-powered bicycle blender to make smoothies out of the very ingredients found in Burt's Bees products. If you wanted a honey almond raspberry shake, you could whisk one up while getting a short burst of good old cardio, no electricity needed. The notion on the rational product side was simple: If you wouldn't put it in you, don't put it on you. The smoothie stations were effective demonstrations of that mantra. The truth is, Burt's Bees products are so natural that you can eat them. I don't usually recommend it because, of course, they're not made to taste good. But all in all, "Find Your Burt" was a complete demonstration of Burt's Bees' core beliefs, values, and products, all centered around on co-creation with its new and dedicated customers.

All told, zero media dollars were spent and the campaign ended up drawing more than sixty-three million media impressions, including coverage from *The Today Show*, *Good Morning America*, and many different outlets. It was chosen as the Small Agency Campaign of the Year by *Ad Age*, which was a fabulous honor. But most importantly, the campaign was a proof of principle about our beliefs in collaboration and co-creation at Baldwin&. We continued to work with Burt's Bees for years after that campaign, which was an absolute joy because they approached their business model in the same manner.

If something didn't fit with the company's beliefs, or they weren't comfortable with a certain decision, they would tell you and hold themselves to their own very high standards. Every decision Burt's Bees made was based on the company's beliefs, and those beliefs were always on full display. "Good for you, good for us, good for all" wasn't just a catchy marketing phrase we collaborated with Burt's Bees to create; it's an honest articulation of their "Greater Good" business model.

Ben & Jerry's Also Gets It

Millennials and iGen won't buy from companies they believe are unethical, but there's also a healthy skepticism of companies attempting to market products in an "ethical" but inauthentic way. Is it real, or is it an act to manipulate consumers (there's that word again)? And make no mistake, they will find out if you're BS-ing them.

When it comes to Ben & Jerry's, rest assured they are not faking living their beliefs. Doing good is built into the company's business model. They didn't stop and say, "OK, we've got this delicious ice cream, so how can we sell it by doing positive things?" They said the reverse: "Hey, we want to do positive things, so how can we use our products to make a difference? Ice cream's the thing we're going to produce."

Over the years, Ben & Jerry's has weighed into politics, feminism, and social issues. They produce special flavors of ice cream, like Rainforest Crunch and Empower Mint, that raise money for specific causes. The delicious brownies that fill pints of Half Baked come from New York's Greyston Bakery, which employs ex-convicts, homeless, and other people on hard times in need of employment. Could they get cheaper brownies from another bakery? Sure, but it would go against their core values and beliefs. Doing good goes in every direction at Ben & Jerry's.

State Street: Almost Perfect

State Street is one of the oldest financial services companies in the United States, but it attracted quite a bit of attention in early 2017 with the unveiling of its "Fearless Girl" statue on Wall Street in New York City. The statue, which depicts a young girl confidently staring down the well-known "Charging Bull" statue, quickly became a phenomenon.[20]

It was widely reported on by media outlets and became an overnight sensation, drawing parents and their daughters in massive numbers. The statue was meant to inspire gender equality and diversity in the workplace, and it included a plaque that read, "Know the power of women in leadership. SHE makes a difference." As the father of a daughter, the narrative State Street created is one I could happily get behind.

The celebration was short-lived for some, however, after it was revealed State Street, despite campaigning for equal treatment and pay of women in the workplace, failed to pay their own female employees a salary equal to that of their male employees. There was a small but immediate backlash, and understandably so.[21]

State Street was trying to do the right thing, but it had a bit of a misstep because it didn't see the larger picture. Advertising yourself as belief-driven when you're not firing at 100 percent is a surefire way to draw people's ire. Giving a damn must be built into your business model. Otherwise, people will sniff it out.

Let's applaud State Street for the idea. It deserves massive kudos for the brilliantly simple execution, which has had an overwhelmingly positive effect throughout the country. I might be nitpicking, but imagine, in addition to the statue, if the company also had made a commitment to address pay inequalities among its own employees. My goodness, can you imagine how overwhelmingly positive, and bulletproof, the reception would have been?

Building from the Bottom Up

Baldwin& is in the process of re-creating a brand for Seventh Generation called "Rooted Beauty." Building a brand from the bottom up offers the best opportunity to bake your values and beliefs into the brand at the very level of the business model. Seventh Generation, a green cleaning company, prioritizes sustainability in everything it does, so the same mentality had to be reflected in Rooted Beauty.

Rooted Beauty was started by Kim Garrett with the intention of having a one-to-one, impactful relationship with women in need, burdened by extreme poverty, abuse, or sex trafficking. This is accomplished through product-assigned microfunding, meaning every time you buy a Rooted Beauty product, a percentage of that product's profits go into a fund to help a specific woman in another part of the country.

Once she is fully funded, the profits then go into another microfund for a different woman. Each fund is unique, so you might be helping someone buy a sewing machine to start a business, or get training, or pay needed legal fees. The point is to create ongoing impact.

Capitalism versus Connected Capitalism

By attaching profit to the simple idea of making good

things happen for people, we can transform the world. That's the driving force behind connected capitalism. When a company stops seeing people as consumers and begins seeing them as collaborators or participants, it completely changes its orientation. When you're collaborating with people to make a great product that does good things, it's a wildly different approach than looking at the world with the sole intention of making money and satisfying shareholders.

If you're reading this and thinking to yourself, "That's great and all, David, but won't people just buy the best product? Isn't that the free market at work?" Well, yes and no, and we only need to look to airlines as an example. Airlines have continued to put profits ahead of user experience to a point where leg room, which used to be a commodity, is now a premium. By the way, I'll bet almost everyone you know now hates flying. Coincidence?

By attaching profit to the simple idea of making good things happen for people, we can transform the world.

That's capitalism at work, and as we've established, out-of-control capitalism is the cancery goodness of growth for the sake of growth. The ironic part about the grow-at-all-costs mentality is, it actually drives jobs out of the United States. In the coldhearted, greed-is-good model of capitalism, why would you pay a person a fair wage when you can exploit someone else abroad and get it cheaper? The answer of course is, you wouldn't, and so the jobs get outsourced.

Connected capitalism is a rejection of those notions and acceptance of tying all of the strings together to do good. Make money. Do good. Win-win.

Creating Shared Value

The key to succeeding in connected capitalism begins with creating Shared Value with your customers. What is Shared Value, you ask? Shared Value—not to be confused with shared values—is a concept created by Harvard Business School professor Michael Porter, who defined it as "capitalism as it was meant to be" in his 2013 TED Talk. "It's not incrementally competing for trivial differences in products, attributes, and market share," Porter added. "It's social value plus economic value simultaneously."[22]

Here's a hypothetical example put forward by Eric Schlosser in the book *Fast Food Nation: The Dark Side of the All-American Meal.* If McDonald's wanted to solve the issues caused by factory farming, it could do so almost overnight. A company like McDonald's wields such economic power that if it decided it wanted to shift away from the large, industrial farms that sacrifice animal welfare for the bottom line and instead serve cruelty-free, pasture-raised beef, the rest of the fast food industry would have to follow. Sure, it might raise the price of Big Macs and Quarter Pounders by ten cents, but in the growing Belief Economy, it's a price people would be willing to absorb for something authentically good.

That would be a massively influential decision with a positive impact, although there are always examples from the other end of the spectrum. Take Papa John's, for instance. Back in 2012, its CEO announced publicly that customers were going to have to pay an additional fourteen cents on every pizza to cover the increased cost of health insurance for the company's employees after the implementation of the Affordable Care Act. That was met with widespread criticism, although it had less to do with the slight price increase and more to do with the company effectively stating, "We don't value our employees enough to cover their health insurance. We're going to make you do it." It was a bad look for a company that could have easily afforded the extra cost.[23]

Capitalism is a push-and-pull system. The pull is the demand for whatever product or service your company provides, and the push is the supply you provide. That makes sense, right? It's fairly basic economics at play.

Connected capitalism, on the other hand, is more like a push and pull plus one. While you're still pushing out your product or service as you would in traditional capitalism, the demand isn't just for said product or service; it also includes an emotional component.

Now, Porter's idea of Shared Value is a hotly debated topic, and there are examples of how it can fail, particularly when a company ignores traditional corporate social responsibility (CSR) efforts at the expense of a Shared Value philosophy. But when CSR and Shared Value work in concert, the effects can be quite powerful. Social media and e-commerce are also changing the value equations put forth in the original article, but that's exactly why advertising, design, and marketing are so important to the topic and the process. We can play a crucial role in creating an extra dimension of Shared Value.[24]

Greenwashing: The Kind of Washing that Makes You Feel Dirty

This is a great opportunity to talk about Greenwashing, also known as Goodwashing or, ironically, Badwashing. This is when a company, at best, tries to communicate what we in the business refer to as "a big load of crap" about an issue or cause that isn't based on any sort of reality. At worst, companies actually outright lie about their CSR

> **Greenwashing is when a company communicates what we in the business refer to as "a big load of crap."**

efforts or are disingenuous in their communications. There are numerous examples of this, but one that stands out is when certain companies in the skin care category tout their "natural ingredients," when the truth is, those ingredients are used only in trace amounts while the rest of the formula is full of ineffectual or even harmful ingredients.

From a marketing standpoint, it's quite dangerous. Remember, millennials and iGen are wary of insincere marketing messages, and they are adept at sniffing them out. They do their homework and *will* reject brands they believe are blindly marketing to sell products without any deeper meaning. Seventy percent of millennials and iGen, however, will back brands that support causes. There's a really wonderful distinction to be made here.

When a brand has an authentic belief system that squarely connects with people beyond the what and into the why of its product, and it lives at a values level inside the company, that's the sweet spot. If a brand can genuinely demonstrate the positive impact it makes beyond simply selling a product, it can attract passionate followers, advocates, and collaborators. And that's the name of the game in the Belief Economy.

CHAPTER 3 HIGHLIGHTS

A quick look back at the most salient takeaways from chapter 3:

- **Connected capitalism at its core:** A free-market economy needs private business owners, but the Belief Economy needs owners who create business models around the bottom line *and* doing good. Profit isn't the only concern in connected capitalism.

- **Creating Shared Value:** According to Harvard Business School professor Michael Porter, Shared Value is creating "social value plus economic value simultaneously," or in other words, "capitalism as it was meant to be."

- **Authenticity matters:** Greenwashing, the act of misrepresenting, or worse, outright lying about your brand's CSR efforts or beliefs, will doom you in the eyes of millennials and iGen. They simply don't tolerate insincerity.

CHAPTER 4

WHY YOU SHOULD THINK OF YOUR BRAND AS A VERB.

While there's no universal definition of the term *Belief-Driven Brand*, we've adopted a simple description at Baldwin&: a brand that stands for something *beyond* the functional benefits of what it makes or does. Of course, a brand will always strive to improve its product, but one driven by belief will seek to better its product while simultaneously creating Shared Value, connecting with people through shared values and emotions, and tying all of its actions into a core belief system. Essentially, a brand *is* behavior.

Belief-Driven Brands are earned over time, giving you an emotional credibility nearly impossible to place a value on. Passion, purpose, and impact can't be faked; we've already established millennials and iGen are particularly adept at sniffing out insincerity. Instead, a brand must come from a genuine place of why—*Why* does our company do what it does? *Why* does it matter? A brand's focus can't be solely on the product. News flash: Even the hottest, must-have products are replicated by competing brands within months. Virtually every snack, drink, gadget, tool, and device you can think of can be copied, so brands must go deeper.

What it all boils down to is authenticity. Belief-Driven Brands are authentic in their beliefs and with the message they broadcast to people. True authenticity is quite brave.

Every brand says it wants to be authentic, but many will turn right around and BS you. A Belief-Driven Brand won't.

Belief-Driven Brands versus Passion Brands

To trace the history of the Belief-Driven Brand, we have to talk about what is often referred to as a Passion Brand. A logical starting point to understanding Passion Brands might be the car culture that emerged in the 1950s and '60s. Pontiac GTOs, Ford Mustangs, Chevrolet Camaros—these cars represented so much more to their drivers than a simple machine capable of getting them from point A to point B. They stood for street racing and the open road, Route 66 and the wind blowing through your hair. For those who owned them, those cars became part of their identity.

Passion, purpose, and impact can't be faked.

Gibson guitars is another great example of a Passion Brand. When most people think about electric guitars, two brands immediately come to mind: Gibson and Fender. Gibson was founded right around the turn of the twentieth century and has been ubiquitous in the music industry in the subsequent one hundred-plus years. When a musician picks up a Gibson, they feel it. Of course they literally hold the guitar in their hands, but they *feel* the fundamental beauty of what it means to play a Gibson. There's a palpable sense of history and tradition in that experience. Many music companies would kill for Gibson's heritage and quality. But it doesn't stand for something bigger than what it makes. It's just really fricking cool, and this has served it well for a long, long time.

Passion Brands thrived at a time when you didn't have to worry as much about what the company itself was up to. Back then, reputation was largely guarded and protected from the inside out. Man, have things changed. That era is coming to an end.

Belief-Driven Brands Are Fueled by Belief Systems

Many brands have embraced the values- and purpose-driven attitude that defines the Belief-Driven Brand. Some are major international companies (e.g., Nike, Dove), while others are smaller in scale (e.g., REI, Patagonia), but they all share something in common: their concerns extend beyond simply selling products and making money.

Nike is a perfect example of a Passion Brand that has transformed into a Belief-Driven Brand. Since the late 1980s, Nike has been using three simple words ("Just Do It") to convey the message of its belief system: Everyone has a winner inside of them. Striving for your best and attempting to achieve greatness isn't reserved solely for elite athletes. Whether you're a rec league superstar, a gym regular, or a once-in-a-blue-moon jogger, you can share the same emotional feeling that the world's greatest athletes experience during competition.

> **Essentially, a brand is behavior.**

Back in 2012, Nike released what many consider to be its finest TV commercial, and still stands as one of my personal all-time favorites. The commercial, titled, "Find Your Greatness," starts with a distant figure slowly moving toward the camera. As the figure gets closer and begins to come into focus, you see it's an overweight boy jogging. As we watch him move closer, the voice-over narration goes into a short, one-minute manifesto on the concept of greatness: what it is, what it isn't, and who can attain it (hint: everyone). "Greatness is not some rare DNA strand, not some precious thing," the narrator tells us. "Greatness is no more unique to us than breathing. We're all capable of it. All of us." It's such a simple yet effective message. The commercial isn't overly stuffed with flashy graphics or cameos from famous athletes. In fact, it's completely devoid of those. It's just a simple one-shot on a kid trying to change himself for the better, a kid trying to find his greatness.

This belief system has permeated Nike for decades. "Just

Do It" and "Find Your Greatness" are not just marketing slogans; they are mantras that reflect the brand's values and beliefs. Nike's passion is reflected in its customers, which are among the most loyal in the world,[25] and the evolving way the company does business.

The steady increase in the number of Belief-Driven Brands in recent years has corresponded with a decreasing emphasis on the evolving approach of positioning, which refers to how people see and distinguish between different brands. Positioning has been viewed as marketing gospel since the mid-1900s, but is it starting to change?

Positioning versus Point of View

The concept of positioning is widely credited to Al Ries and Jack Trout, two marketing gurus who championed the idea in the 1960s and '70s. Best of all, you don't have to be an expert in the field to understand the premise behind the concept. Imagine every single product category is its own ladder.[26] The various brands selling a given product are positioned accordingly on each ladder by the economic power they wield. The ladders aren't top-heavy; only two or three brands can occupy the top few rungs. This concept is called laddering (clever name, right?).

A brand's positioning is where it fits on the ladder, which

is a symbol for the marketplace. Is it near the top or on a lower rung working its way up? This method of evaluation still has its benefits, but it used to be more prominent. The question is, can a brand's values, belief systems, actions, and behaviors create a new distinctiveness that goes beyond traditional positioning?

My friend and colleague Dan Carlton, who runs a strategic practice called The Paragraph Project in Durham, North Carolina, recently wrote a white paper titled, "The Death of Positioning." In it, he specifically highlighted Avis, which famously positioned itself as number two in the car rental service. He made the observation that by positioning itself as the second-best option for customers, Avis never made it to number one. In fact, it stayed solidly at number two. It's a fascinating marketing case study. By adopting the "When you're only number two, you try harder" tagline, Avis actually may have limited itself. Yet, this is, and should be, considered an incredibly famous, effective campaign. Why?

First of all, the work was groundbreaking and brilliant. But I'd also argue that what Avis unequivocally accomplished was to create an ethos, a belief system, and a point of view that permeated the entire company. "We try harder" wasn't just a catchy marketing slogan; it was the attitude of every employee. That's the Belief Economy in action *before* the Belief Economy was embraced on a wider level. It's an important example of how brands can market today by taking a stand and embracing a point of view in the world, in the process replacing the age-old unique selling proposition (USP).

USP, which dates back to the 1960s and advertising legend Rosser Reeves, is the concept of identifying the unique difference in your product that would convince customers to switch brands. If you study advertising from the era, you'll notice it's typically focused on one specific ingredient, benefit, or other differentiator. Those days are over. Brands can take a stand and build themselves around an authentic ethos to make themselves more distinctive rather than a USP to remain relevant.

Don't Sacrifice Quality

That being said, the product is still crucial. Brands fail every day because of poor products. There's an old advertising adage attributed to Doyle Dane Bernbach that says, "Great advertising will kill a bad product." What does that mean, you ask? You can get anyone to buy something once, but if their experience with the product is negative, they may never buy it again. It is infinitely harder to resell an inferior product.

In fact, everything we've discussed up until this point (and beyond) assumes your brand is selling a winning product. If that's not the case, you have to do everything you can to make your product great.

The cost of entry is a winning product, and by winning product I don't necessarily mean a Seth Godin "purple cow," which is something truly one of a kind and revolutionary. Honey Maid, for instance, makes and sells graham crackers, and it has done so for decades. Everyone loves graham crackers, but let's be honest, they're hardly a revolutionary, life-changing product. If you lined up Honey Maid with ten other competitors and did a blind taste test, most probably couldn't tell the difference. But Honey Maid still sells a *good* product. Your brand must do the same.

How Your Brand Will Change

Giving a damn is essential for brands in the growing Belief Economy, but how does it change your brand?

This is all in no way suggesting you forgo your daily marketing activity, promotions, campaigns, and other pushes. We're actually talking about making them even more powerful by creating a lens led by your point of view to give them more focus.

There's a tremendous amount of cultural power that permeates a company that lives and breathes its own values. It's not only imperative as part of a company's business model, but it also energizes the internal culture. We know millennials and iGen are entering the workforce in major numbers over the next ten-plus years, and they want to work at companies where they can make a genuine impact. By giving a damn, embracing your beliefs, and considering the long-term impact of your actions, your company immediately becomes more appealing to the motivated individuals of the youngest generations.

John Replogle, the former CEO of Burt's Bees, current CEO of Seventh Generation, and, as you might recall, the author of this book's foreword, is a major proponent of connected capitalism. His research has shown there are five aspirations rooted within human needs and desires that define the priorities and behaviors of millennials and iGen. These aspirations highlight the path connected capitalism will open to the marketplace of the future:

- *Abundance without waste*: More experiences with fewer resources
- *Truly as you are*: Welcoming imperfection as honest and beautiful
- *Get closer*: Connecting with the people behind the brand promise

- *All of it*: Expecting freedom from binaries and finish lines
- *Do some good*: Having a positive impact in the everyday world

Too often, brands sacrifice long-term commitment and vision for short-term gains. This is a mistake, but it's often convenient and almost always addictive. The most successful Belief-Driven Brands use their values as an avenue to create a positive conversation and generate activation among people without, for lack of a better term, prostituting themselves out. Are there brands out there that will just spend, spend, and spend some more to find success? Of course, but it's lazy. Why not try to be better? Why not go beyond standard marketing practice? Why not try to spend a little bit less and simply outsmart your competition with more clever and engaging marketing?

When a brand is laying out its values and creating its core beliefs, it's important to define what it stands for. But it's equally as important to clearly define what it does *not* stand for. This tension isn't inherently negative. In fact, it's actually empowering and positive. "We're against waste," or "We're against negativity." These aren't negative in outcome.

Walking the Walk

Patagonia, Inc. is an example of a Belief-Driven Brand that has not only stated what it stands for but also what it stands against. The company, which sells sustainable outdoor clothing, ran an amazing campaign around Christmas in 2011. The idea was simple: It urged customers *not* to buy a specific jacket. Confused? No, Patagonia wasn't trying to sell less; it was trying to sell more responsibly. The idea behind the "Don't Buy This Jacket" campaign was to urge customers to buy a new jacket *only* if they actually needed it. Additionally, the company offered to repair your current jacket rather than throw it out.

The campaign wasn't just a marketing ploy for Patagonia but instead aligned with the core value of the company: Don't be wasteful. If you don't need to buy a new jacket, don't buy one. But if you do need a new one, we're happy to sell you this fantastic one. All of this was part of its Common Threads Initiative, which encouraged people to buy only what they needed, when they needed it, and to recycle or reuse what they already had. Talk about living your values and core belief system. Many companies would be too scared to run an ad saying, "Don't buy this product," during the holiday season, but Patagonia embraces its ethos.

Then we have Recreational Equipment, Inc., more

commonly known as REI, a company that sells outdoor recreational gear, including sporting goods, camping equipment, and clothing. It ran a 2015 campaign called "#OptOutside" that was as simple as it was effective. The company decided Black Friday, the lovely, nightmarish shopping day immediately following Thanksgiving, was a perfect day to close all of its stores and encourage its customers and employees to go outside. Confused again? Well, this isn't a study in traditional marketing techniques.

REI wasn't concerned with its sales on a single day of the year. The company hires people who truly love the outdoors because, quite simply, this action directly aligns with its belief system. REI wants the people selling its equipment to love, use, and understand the merchandise themselves. Closing the stores for the busiest shopping day of the year so the employees can live the company's ethos is a beautiful example of REI living its values.

In the past, great advertising centered on insights reflecting some powerful customer truths. Today, instead, you can actually affect customer truths.

CHAPTER 4 HIGHLIGHTS

A quick look back at the most salient takeaways from chapter 4:

- **You've got to believe:** Belief-Driven Brands are brands that stand for something beyond the functional benefits of the products they make or services they provide. They are the lifeblood of the Belief Economy.

- **Point of view versus positioning:** Can having a point of view based on a powerful, authentic belief system replace the traditional practice of positioning yourself in the marketplace?

- **Brands are behavior:** By embracing your beliefs and weighing the long-term impact of your actions, your brand can become more appealing to the motivated individuals of the two youngest generations.

DON'T CHECK YOUR HUMANITY AT THE DOOR; YOU'LL NEED IT AT THE OFFICE.

For some reason, particularly in marketing departments and advertising agencies, people forget they're people. They make assumptions that the public is there to be hunted like big game for their "sale," and they'll do anything to make that sale. But when they walk out the door to go home, they become humans again, motivated by the things humans are motivated by: love, fear, desire, envy. You know, human stuff.

This has to change. We can no longer let our humanity-door hit us in the ass when we leave our home to go to work. We have to orient our brands, our activities, and our communications in a much more human way.

The future is in the hands of millennials and iGen. We've already established this fact, but it simply can't be overstated. Brands must not only understand but also embrace the growing Belief Economy.

Think about it this way: Who is going to work for your company in the immediate and near futures? Who is going to move into management roles within your company over the next decade or so? Millennials and iGen.

Without a defined belief system, core values, and point of view, your company may be surpassed by its competitors. The Belief Economy permeates a company's culture from the bottom up. It isn't just reflected in the people buying the product but also in the people making, selling, packaging, and distributing the product, too. It's simple: millennials are starting to run the show, iGen coming right behind them, and the Belief Economy isn't going anywhere. Brands that don't understand this may be in deep trouble. But that doesn't have to be *your* brand.

Your Belief-Driven Path

Every brand has its own path to becoming a Belief-Driven Brand. That's important, so I'll repeat it: Every single brand can become a Belief-Driven Brand in its own way. There is an entry point into the Belief Economy for every brand under the sun. The trick, of course, is following the right path.

Generally speaking, there are two different routes brands can take to become Belief-Driven. They can choose to be a genuine Belief-Driven Brand by fully committing to their core values from the business-model level up; we'll call this living like a saint. Or they can start smaller by choosing to do one thing that has a positive impact on the world, or solving a simple problem for their customer based on their ethos.

Think of it this way: You can start from your business

model up (Burt's Bees) or your advertising down (Dove), which can actually begin to affect your business model over time. The path you choose doesn't matter as long as you pick one and move forward.

The first step on the chosen path has to be identifying your brand's reason for existing, and that reason has to be authentic. This can seem daunting at first, but once you can articulate it, it's incredibly powerful. Burt's Bees, for instance, exists because "nature needs a champion." Simple. Powerful. Authentic. Once its reason for existing was established, it opened a door to a world of behavior, communication, and people that aligned with its core vision of the brand.

The reason you give a damn becomes your point of difference.

Remember, your brand is a verb instead of a noun. Brands are a set of behaviors based on an authentic belief system. More often than not, a brand's reason for existing has become fossilized, buried under years of corporate jargon or internal marketing documents. If that's the case, put on your archaeologist hat and get digging. This is the beginning of the process at Baldwin& when we collaborate with clients looking to reconnect with their original reasons to be. We interview executives and employees. We talk to the founder, if they're still alive. If not, we have to do some deeper forensics: What impact does your company currently have and what impact can it have in the future? What are you trying to do? What do you hope happens in the world because of your company and the product it sells?

By answering these questions, you can peel back the layers on your brand like an onion until you boil the essence down to one or two words. There's an inherent beauty in authentically connecting with what your brand is and what it stands for. It also eliminates the need for a USP, because the reason you give a damn *becomes* your point of difference. Your brand's unique belief system will separate you from the competition. If you're Apple and you've created the iPod, well, great for you. You've created a product that will revolutionize the world. Most brands aren't so fortunate, but having a clearly defined point of view helps frame your brand in the minds of others and can reframe whatever benefits you actually have. If their beliefs and values align with yours, they may start to give you the benefit of the doubt.

#LikeAGirl

One of the most beautiful examples of a Belief-Driven Brand creating collaboration through Shared Value is Always' "#LikeAGirl" campaign, which was launched back in 2014. When you think about advertising for feminine hygiene products, there's a rich montage of terrible commercials spanning decades. You know what I'm referring to. It might be a mother and a daughter in a canoe, or in a car, or in their house, and the daughter asks, "Do you ever have that not-so-fresh feeling?" From there, we might be treated to the highly scientific test showing blue liquid pouring into the different products. It was out of gas, and Always realized it had an opportunity to tap into a different emotional wavelength: confidence. Enter #LikeAGirl.

In a series of videos tied into the campaign, women and men were instructed to "throw like a girl." The results were predictably exaggerated throwing motions and clichéd movements. On the second time through, the same people were told to consciously forget the clichés and preconceived notions they already had in their minds. "How would a girl really throw a baseball?" they were asked. The results were completely different.

The campaign phrase became a rallying cry around confidence for women, and the hashtag #LikeAGirl became wildly popular on social media, allowing people to upload videos of themselves doing things "like a girl." Baseball, karate, gardening, science projects—the user-generated videos covered everything.

From a business-model standpoint, Always didn't have to change anything. This is a brand that has always been useful to women, but now they could just celebrate and champion women. They used advertising and social media to connect with people and cocreate action through their shared values.

Start Small, but Just Start

Remember, you *typically* can't become a Belief-Driven Brand overnight. I say typically because that's usually not how it works, although there are instances of overnight sensations. Apple's legendary "1984" commercial forever changed the trajectory of Super Bowl advertising and helped establish them as a major player in the technology world. But again, that's Apple, a company constantly engineering revolutions. The rest of us might have to be more patient.

"Belief-Driven Brand" is a badge of honor that takes commitment, consistency, and, most importantly, time to earn. There's just no way around this. You must exhibit a consistency of behavior over time. You can't just talk the talk; you've got to walk the walk.

Your behavior doesn't have to be a major overhaul or sweeping company-wide change, but it does have to be authentic. If you start with something small that resonates with people and validate it through social media interactions, you'll begin a snowball effect. That simple proof of concept can precipitate a larger change within your company.

> **There are two great times to plant an oak tree: twenty years ago and today.**

But when should a brand plan to join this blossoming Belief Economy? Allow me to answer the question with an old saying: *There are two great times to plant an oak tree: twenty years ago and today.* In other words, even if you've squandered recent years by not building your brand, all is not lost. But you should begin taking steps to become a Belief-Driven Brand right now. You can't afford to continue waiting.

Understanding Advertising's Role

If I could change anything about this crazy business we're in, it would be the notion that advertising is a silver bullet you can use to magically create success. Silver bullets are, by definition, incredibly rare. If advertising were a silver bullet, everyone would be number one. So when a client approaches me and says, "I'm going to put everything into this one piece of work," but they've neglected their brand for years or haven't changed their product experience, I cringe. I get it; it's tempting. It's damn tempting, in fact. Even if that one thing does work, you still have to create consistent behavior based on your belief system over time.

Everyone wants to be the next Dollar Shave Club, a relatively unknown company (but one with a defined belief system) that exploded after an effectively simple advertising video starring its founder went viral. But what was really going on is that their business model turned the entire category on its head. Watch the video and you'll see a textbook example of talking to the Belief Economy. The founder lays out a very strong belief system about the current state of the razor blade industry and the company's role in it.

If advertising were a silver bullet, everyone would be number one.

Instead of focusing on hitting nothing but viral home runs with advertising, you have to focus on your own beliefs, values, and behaviors. Along with sound fundamentals, those are the ingredients that will help the oak tree grow strong over time.

Advertising, selling, and marketing are part art, part science, but the science is quickly catching up. Data are collected by more websites than we can count, and include social mega-powers like Google, Facebook, Twitter, Snapchat, and Instagram. Those data collection algorithms aren't yet smart enough to know *exactly* what we want as customers. In five years, who knows? But right now, it isn't quite there yet. For instance, if my friend starts a company that makes boots and I like his page on Facebook, I will start seeing ads for boots on my page. Artificial intelligence (AI) doesn't know I'm not looking for boots. I'm just supporting my friend. That's one of the flaws not yet addressed.

The algorithms are constantly evolving. There's no way to know what the future holds twenty-plus years from now. In the immediate to near future, however, there's an opportunity to be coconspirators with people through your advertising. Don't just talk at them; remember, they're not consumers. Instead, allow them to cocreate with you. Change your mindset from "To whom are we selling today?" to "With whom are we collaborating today?" This is a much richer territory for an advertising agency to speak from and opens up a completely different conversation with people. And, dare I say, this just might be the future of advertising.

What We Know

Successful advertising intertwines intuition with the insights gained from data collection, but it will always be imperfect. This is true for most entertainment media. Almost every commercial you see on TV and film you watch in the theaters was received well in focus groups. Yet the reality is, most TV advertising sucks and most films perform below expectations at the box office. If testing is reliable, why is this the case? Where's the breakdown? Well, for one, focus groups can't always accurately reflect the larger public, and two, understanding what people are thinking is difficult. If advertisers or film studios could accurately predict the outcomes of their projects, they would. Every. Single. Time.

Peter Field, in association with the Institute of Practitioners of Advertising, found creatively awarded campaigns are eleven times more efficient at generating market share increase. "Creatively awarded campaigns were much more certain to achieve that result. The less creative campaigns were not only less efficient, but also less predictable than the creatively awarded ones. This suggests a departure from the conventional wisdom that a more creative approach is the 'riskier' one."[27] This makes sense, right? Playing it safe may actually be a riskier approach, because you're more apt to bore people. When you play it safe, you may actually end up wasting money. This is such a contradiction that it's a bit hard to get your head around, but it's true.

When you play it safe, you may actually end up wasting money.

James Hurman, in a 2011 study titled, *The Case for Creativity*, looked at the stock value growth for Cannes Advertisers of the Year between 2000 and 2009, compared to the S&P 500 annual average. His findings were fascinating. "Cannes Advertiser of the Year experienced on average 41% stock value growth in the year they won the award. The S&P 500 experienced a fraction of that growth at 0.5%. Further analysis revealed in each case the winning companies had been going through a period of greater focus on creativity and innovation throughout their business, of which award-winning advertising and stock market success where symptomatic."

Given this information and the overwhelming evidence that focus groups don't automatically translate to success, the obvious follow-up question is, why do brands still use focus groups? Like much of the advertising world, it dates back to Rosser Reeves and the giants from the 1950s and '60s. These testing methods have their benefits as predictive models, *but they don't always lead to better advertising.* Generally speaking, the bigger the company, the more institutionalized those pre- and post-testing types can be.

What We Don't Know

Specific advertisements and commercials are unpredictable. It's just impossible to know, beyond the shadow of a doubt, what will resonate and to what degree. It's impossible to know what video will go viral next. If it weren't, there would be a new one every day, created by a brand.

That's why a brand's authentic point of view is so important. As long as your message is based on something real, important, and impactful, people will care about it. The emotional resonance will trump all of the blindly gathered data. The best comparison is something humans have tried to understand for their entire existence: love. There's no science to support the person you fall in love with. The match.coms of the world boast about their compatibility algorithms, but those are far from perfect. Love is impossible to predict.

It's the same thing with poetry or art. There's no universal way to quantify or evaluate those entities across public opinion. What someone scoffs at, someone else could find genius. Can you imagine putting something as personal as poetry through testing? Suddenly, you're changing every other word, or the structure, and you've lost the original message.

Most people mistakenly think an advertiser's job is to jam

a message into your head with a crowbar. Do you want your message to resonate? Of course, but think about it this way: if you walk into a party, you don't just start screaming and yelling so everyone there hears your message. Advertising is no different. Yelling to convey your message will only turn people off. There's a way to do it that's pleasant and creates a real connection with people. People might say they hate advertising, but everyone has a favorite commercial. People *love* advertising when it's great.

Beliefs Unite Us

A brand's avenue for conveying its message may change with each new commercial or advertisement, but as long as the message itself is genuine and consistent with the brand's beliefs and behaviors, like-minded people will take notice. People have a habit of clustering together into tribes based on shared values and beliefs. Many advertising agencies like to take credit for these "movements," but this is a major pet peeve of mine. Civil rights, women's suffrage, Black Lives Matter—these are movements. A few hundred thousand people (and I'm being kind with that number) in a country of nearly 330 million people creating a sense of community around a specific product and/or message is far different from creating a movement. It's important to remember that distinction.

While brands typically don't create movements on their own, they can motivate customers to take action. Howard Gossage once said, "People don't read advertising. They read things they're interested in." At the time, he was talking about print ads, but the sentiment still rings true in today's digital world. The number one enemy of advertisers today is the Skip button. You typically have a three- to five-second window to capture a person's attention before they'll be tempted to hit the Skip button. Again, people like to say they hate advertising, but they're all experts at quickly identifying the narrative of a commercial and deciding whether it appeals to them.

The number one enemy of advertisers today is the Skip button.

Here's one you can relate to. If it's a drug commercial with a talking head, you might immediately look to the timer on the Skip button. But if it's something new or interesting, you might stick with it a little bit longer. It's a tough, tough place to be as an advertiser, that's for sure, but this much will always be true: a magnetic piece of content is a magnetic piece of content. It doesn't matter where that content appears or how it's engaged; if it's something worth watching, people will watch.

If you have trouble thinking of your customers as people

instead of consumers, just use yourself as a guide. After all, *you* are a human being, too. You're not a number on a spreadsheet. Consider your own perspective on advertising and what it means to you in your daily life. Do you ignore the bad stuff that yells at you or wall-to-wall information about things you don't care about? What are your own values and how do they affect your shopping habits and decisions?

People will connect with brands they share values with, but don't pretend people want to be friends with brands. They don't. They want your brand to add value to their life. Think of it this way: Almost everyone has headphones, but would you want to be friends with a headphones company that advertises across your Facebook page? Of course not. That doesn't add any value to your life. Now, if that company served you a unique piece of content or idea that appealed to you and opened the door for you to connect with them, well, that's a different story.

Conventional wisdom says that at any given time, about 5 percent of the advertising in America is quite good, while the other 95 percent is terrible, annoying, or downright awful. That was true fifty years ago, and it remains true today. What is changing is the level of tenacity with which brands cling to the old rules of advertising. More and more brands are breaking free from the institutional chains of yesteryear and embracing a different mindset. Is it more important to you to do whatever it takes to ace testing or to take a stand and do what's right for your customer?

CHAPTER 5 HIGHLIGHTS

A quick look back at the most salient takeaways from chapter 5:

- **Every brand has a path:** Whether it's committing to your core values at the business-model level or starting smaller by making a positive impact on the world, every single brand has a path toward becoming a Belief-Driven Brand.

- **Forget any shortcuts:** "Belief-Driven Brand" is a badge of honor that takes commitment, consistency, and, of course, time to earn. There's no way around this. Brands are fulfilled over time.

- **There are no silver bullets:** Advertising is unpredictable and works best when based on a truth. This makes your brand's authentic point of view critical. If your message is based on something real and impactful, the right people will care about it.

YOU DON'T HAVE TO LIVE LIKE A SAINT TO SAVE THE WORLD.

Many brands embrace their values and beliefs and use them to navigate the growing Belief Economy. Many Belief-Driven Brands have their values baked into their business model. Other brands fall short of a true Belief-Driven designation but still try to make things better. But there are also a segment of brands out there trying to figure out where they fit in the Belief Economy.

You don't have to make the world better, but honestly, if you had the chance to, why wouldn't you?

"This sounds too lofty and aspirational." "What impact can my brand truly have?" "Why does all of this even matter?"

I've heard these questions before. Look, is it possible for a brand to succeed without embracing its beliefs and values and rejecting this notion of the Belief Economy? Yes, it's possible, but these brands will have to significantly outspend their competition. Money is a powerful thing, and it can help a brand succeed through brute force. But why? Why would you willingly reject the opportunity to make things better and connect with the people buying your products on a more personal level?

Being a part of the Belief Economy doesn't mean you have to live a saintly existence like dedicated Belief-Driven Brands. As shown many times already, this isn't about adopting a cause or doing cause marketing for your brand. Some brands are saints and some aren't, and that's completely OK. Creating an authentic belief system doesn't have to be centered on saving kittens. It can be something as simple as striving to deliver a better customer experience that solves a problem relevant to their lives. The point is to have a tangible impact. You don't have to make the world better, but honestly, if you had the chance to, why wouldn't you?

Small Brands Can Think Big

Let's use Funyuns, those tasty onion-flavored snacks, as a hypothetical example. Funyuns' product doesn't inherently help the world (that I know of), so what is the value the brand can bring to the table? Well, it can still create value with people. Find a way to do something good. Funyuns has the word *Fun* in the name. What if the difference it can make, using its belief system, is to find new ways to bring fun to the world and give its employees and customers fun experiences otherwise missing during their day? The question becomes how to lead with these beliefs and make them tangibly real for people. Just because the product it makes doesn't have a far-reaching positive impact on its own doesn't mean the brand can't.

The core notion of Shared Value is that business is

designed to solve problems. If you think about gigantic corporations such as Exxon, McDonald's, or Walmart, they can all have a profound effect when they want to. Why Exxon, for instance, wouldn't be all-in on renewable sources of energy is beyond me. That change, while not simple to execute, would have profound and far-reaching effects on the world over the next one hundred years. Many companies, particularly the large corporations, are still held hostage by quarterly goals and short-term thinking. If I could wave a magic wand and change anything about our capitalistic economy, it would be eliminating the destructive addiction to short-term results.

Consider this my personal invitation to any brand that believes its product prohibits it from joining the Belief Economy. That's dead wrong. You *absolutely* have permission to add value in some way. In fact, I'd argue if you want to survive, you must create Shared Value. We're entering an enlightened era, where people understand what companies are up to, good or bad.

OK, that sounds great and all, but *how* can my brand do good? To answer that question, you first have to answer a few other ones:

- What's the current state of things in your category?
- What change does the customer seek?

- What can you do to make things better (impact)?
- What's the authentic emotion around what you're trying to do?

These questions will help you identify whom you should talk to, sell to, and collaborate with. From there, you must figure out how to put them all together to make something amazing happen. That's the challenge, but it's a damn fun one to tackle.

Where to Start

For many brands, answering the question of how to do good begins with recognizing the impact they're having on the world. Remember, starting small is OK. Joining the Belief Economy doesn't mean your brand has to dedicate every available resource to saving the world. It's really as simple as using your brand's own unique point of view to have a positive impact. Here are a few specific examples:

- *Panera Bread*: The popular restaurant chain pledged to transition its entire menu to 100 percent clean ingredients by 2017. For a chain the size of Panera to do that is no small feat, but the impact is twofold. First, customers are getting healthier meals. I don't think anyone can argue with the benefit of that. Second, it forces Panera to evaluate its distribution chain. The push-pull of capitalism comes into play here. For a company as successful and prominent as Panera to declare it's transitioning to 100 percent clean ingredients forces distributors, suppliers, and farmers to follow suit. They've got to meet specific certification standards; otherwise, Panera will cut ties with them.

- *Target/Walmart*: Companies like Target and Walmart have such an enormous effect on the power consumption in America, so it was a major development when the latter converted its stores to energy-efficient LED lighting back in 2014.[28] Most Walmart locations are open 24-7, so switching to energy-efficient lighting made a huge positive impact on the power grid.

Restaurant chains like Outback Steakhouse, the largest retailer of Choice beef among US restaurants,[29] have a tremendous influence over their supply chains. If these major corporations came together and said, "Hey, we want to make sure there are no more antibiotics in beef," it would be gone very quickly. It would begin to happen overnight. The major hurdle is that so many of these companies are operating off subsidies, so delivering the cheapest food possible trumps all else.

What about brands that sell products that are, to put it bluntly, bad for you if overconsumed? Soda, for instance, might taste delicious, but it's been proven to have negative effects on your body if overingested.[30] That doesn't prohibit a brand from making a positive impact. Let's take a closer look at a few of these brands.

Pepsi

If you love Pepsi's soda products, that's great. I do, too, but let's be honest, they sell corn syrup, sugar, and formula in water. What they produce isn't inherently good for the world, but that didn't stop them from launching the Pepsi Refresh Project in 2010. It was a wonderful campaign in which Pepsi held contests in communities across the country, using its own marketing budget. The contests allowed people to cocreate with Pepsi by proposing ideas for making their communities better. It gave people a chance to "refresh" their communities.

The campaign was wonderfully received and had a positive impact across the United States, but it also had an unexpected negative side effect for the brand. Pepsi put most of its marketing behind the Refresh Project, abandoning many other marketing initiatives, and it resulted in Pepsi falling behind Diet Coke as the nation's second-most popular soda.

The lesson to be learned here, of course, is to strike a proper balance when it comes to marketing and advertising. Pepsi still deserves a massive amount of credit for being ahead of the curve. They showed that a company's product, in this case a sugary cola, doesn't define them; how they behave in the world does. Pepsi found a Shared Value of "refreshment" and used it to have a positive impact on people and their communities.

For as positive as the Refresh Project campaign was for Pepsi, the much-maligned 2017 ad featuring Kendall Jenner was on the opposite end of the spectrum. It was such a train wreck they had to pull the commercial/video.[31] Pepsi tried to attach itself to Black Lives Matter and other movements in a way that was completely inauthentic. It didn't matter that the brand truly believes in and supports the cause; the commercial was tone-deaf and, to be honest, uncomfortable to watch.

While it was a nightmare for Pepsi, it's a prime example of how vigilant people are toward marketing, particularly millennials and iGen. As we've said, if anything your brand is pushing feels disingenuous or inauthentic, you will get roasted.

Gatorade

Gatorade is a company that sells another form of products made of sugar, water, and electrolytes. I'll leave others to debate the health benefits, but Gatorade launched a brilliant campaign back in 2009 called REPLAY the Series, a program that brought together two high school football teams with a long rivalry.

Gatorade exists to replenish and revitalize athletes in order to get peak performances out of them, so REPLAY the Series was just an extension of that point of view. The teams from Easton, Pennsylvania, and Phillipsburg, New Jersey, played to a 7–7 tie in the annual Fork of the Delaware rivalry game years before, so Gatorade invited those players back to finish the game and declare a winner. Gatorade created a television series around the idea, following the training and preparation of the middle-aged players. It was a great idea and, better yet, great fun. (By the way, Phillipsburg won the rematch 27–12.)

The campaign wasn't a corporate social responsibility (CSR) goal of Gatorade's, nor did the company create some kind of sustainability program for a wider benefit. Instead, it demonstrated how Gatorade could make a deeper impact through its shared values via a simple, yet fascinating, advertising construct. Gatorade believes in giving it your all as an athlete, and through that belief, it helped bring those players' dreams to life in a profound way.

Southwest Airlines

Everyone hates flying, right? It's a hassle getting to the airport, getting through security, and getting on the plane itself. Once you're on the plane, that doesn't even guarantee your transportation to your destination, as we've seen repeated instances of overbooked flights forcefully removing paying passengers from their seats in 2017.

What Southwest has tried to do is democratize flying. Their business model is designed to streamline the process of booking a flight, while making it more accessible to more people due to lower prices. Southwest has tried to take the stress out of flying, and guess what? They're the most on-time airline operating right now.

Southwest's airplanes burn jet fuel like their competitors', so it's not exactly like they're saving the world, but they *are* having a positive effect on their customers from their business model up. That much is undeniable.

Unilever

Unilever, the parent company of Dove, Axe, Hellmann's, and hundreds of other notable brands, is an interesting case study. On the one hand is Dove, which launched the Campaign for Real Beauty back in 2004 to celebrate and inspire confidence in women. As the father of a daughter,

I love seeing Dove strive to change the way we think and talk about marketing to women and girls.

On the other hand, Unilever also owns Axe, which rose to fame due to its overly sexualized commercials. "Wear Axe and you'll get laid," the commercials conveyed to young male viewers. Axe is moving away from those types of ads in an attempt to find a better message. In fact, that shift began in 2016 with a campaign centered around men being comfortable in their own skin. They're following the path set by Dove.

Unilever CEO Paul Polman has said every brand under the Unilever umbrella will have a mission to have a positive social impact. Polman sees the power of the Belief Economy very, very clearly and is fully on board. In fact, Unilever has claimed that "brands with 'purpose' at the heart of their message were growing at twice the rate of other brands across Unilever's portfolio."[32]

Amazon

Everyone knows about Amazon. If you've ever ordered anything online or done holiday e-shopping, you've almost certainly utilized Amazon. In fact, it's the most valuable retailer in the United States and one of the largest companies in the world. It's not exactly an unknown commodity, but as an e-commerce company, there isn't much room for sustainability initiatives in their communications.

Instead, Amazon introduced AmazonSmile, a play on the company's distinctive logo. Through AmazonSmile, customers can purchase products through Amazon as they normally would, but 0.5 percent of the sale price goes to any one of thousands of charities that they choose upon checkout. Simple *and* powerful.

Amazon isn't saving the world, but by creating a mechanism that so simply and beautifully integrates directly into their shopping platform, they've created a personal connection through collaboration with customers: buy products through us, and we'll help you donate to a cause you care about. That is awesome in the old sense of the word.

Amazon also unveiled a wonderful commercial during the 2016 holiday season that featured a priest and an imam, two old friends, coincidentally buying each other knee pads for prayer through Amazon. The commercial helped promote Amazon Prime, the company's premium membership, but its message of inclusion during the holiday season was very powerful. It also did a great job of demonstrating how simple Amazon is to use; both men ordered on their mobile phones with minimal effort.

Ancestry.com

Ancestry.com launched a 2017 video just in time for the Fourth of July, celebrating its core offering, demonstrating its product beautifully, and creating a powerful message of inclusion.

The idea was incredibly simple. We hear different voices read the Declaration of Independence over quick cuts of a multicultural mix of people sitting down, moving around in a yet-to-be-revealed room. Occasionally, we cut to a person who is actually delivering the reading of the document. It's a wonderful mélange of races, genders, and ages of the people who make up the very fabric of America. At the end of the video, we pull back and settle to reveal the people have actually been assembling into the same positions as those in John Trumbull's famous painting of the signing in a perfect re-representation of the event. At the same time, a super reads: "Everyone we've assembled here is descended from a signer of the Declaration of Independence. Ancestry.com. Unlock your past. Inspire your future."

In such divided times, this is an important reminder of our heritage and what makes our country so powerful, all from a company that has never taken such a stand. They obviously believe their product can unite people, families, and Americans.

Nedbank

Banks exist, ostensibly, to support local communities and businesses with money, but we also know they can have a predatory side that hurts those same people and organizations. Banks aren't exactly living like saints, but that didn't stop Nedbank from doing good with nothing but a billboard.

Nedbank, a South Africa-based bank, built a solar-powered billboard that helped power several local buildings, including a school. What a simple yet brilliant idea. Billboards, of course, sit in the same spot all day, every day, so why not harness the hours of sunlight they draw for something positive?

Nedbank created something that literally added value to a finite group of people who needed help. Of course, it also turned into an inspirational piece of content that spread around the world. That's just amazing and further proves a brand doesn't need to save the world to be a part of the Belief Economy.

Heineken

Can a beer do good in the world? Absolutely, and as a founder of a brewery in North Carolina, I'll expound on this from a more personal point of view in the next chapter.

Heineken adopted the tagline "Open Your World" many years ago, and it's under that umbrella that they've done a number of different social experiments.

The "Worlds Apart" experiment is a particularly powerful example of how something as seemingly insignificant as beer can have a profound impact. They brought together different people from different backgrounds and ideologies, and first asked them questions individually. *Who are you? What do you do? What do you believe? What's important to you?*

They then paired people whose views on feminism, climate change, and gender identity differed vastly, and had them work together to build two stools and a bar as they got to know each other through conversation. But just as that conversation was getting comfortable, Heineken interrupted the pairs to show them the individual videos they recorded earlier in the process. It certainly created a number of awkward moments between people with completely conflicting mindsets.

After the videos finished, everyone was offered a choice: walk away from the other person and leave the experiment, or sit down at the bar with them and share a Heineken beer together. They all chose to sit down, share a drink, and continue to get to know each other.

Sure, Heineken "only" sells beer, but that social experiment resulted in a beautiful little film. Through its beer, it got people to open their minds up to other people's beliefs and perspectives. Heineken truly lives its "Open Your World" tagline, and it has the global reach to inspire people across the world.

CHAPTER 6 HIGHLIGHTS

A quick look back at the most salient takeaways from chapter 6:

- **Look inward:** Ask yourself these questions: What's the current state of things in your category? What change does your customer seek? What can you do to make things better? These answers will help guide you.

- **Beliefs over products:** While the product a brand produces matters, it isn't necessary for the product to be inherently good for people (e.g., soda). A brand can still cultivate an authentic belief system and solve a problem for their customers.

- **It's OK to start small:** Some brands live like true saints, while others just try to make a positive impact, no matter how small. Creating an authentic belief system doesn't have to be centered on saving kittens.

HOW TO BECOME A BELIEF-DRIVEN BRAND BY DOING GOOD.

One of the running gags on the HBO show *Silicon Valley* is every single startup company's stated goal of making the world a better place. "We're going to do [fill in the blank], and we're going to save the world while doing [fill in the blank]." This is a perfect example of art imitating life; real companies have been saying the same thing for years.

The difference now is that companies have more tools at their disposal and more opportunities than ever to *actually* make a difference. Whether it's social media, TV, or believe it or not, even billboards, brands can use these tools to create positive change. Ninety-five percent of all advertising sucks, but if executed well, advertising can be not only enjoyed but also loved.

If you can bake your core belief system into your brand at a business-model level, you've hit the sweet spot. True Belief-Driven Brands in the Belief Economy have this in common. Now, even if your brand doesn't have those values instilled at the business-model level, you can still have an impact in the world simply with the way you communicate. That's a welcome change from the past. Advertisers have typically used one of two methods to implant their messages in people's heads: by being disruptive and/or clever, or by just being annoying.

The examples included in this chapter demonstrate true

Belief-Driven Brands doing good. All of the advertising campaigns below had a bigger impact beyond sustainability initiatives or increasing product sales. All of these brands have made connected capitalism part of their mission, and it's reflected in their impact on the world.

> Ninety-five percent of all advertising sucks, but if executed well, advertising can be not only enjoyed but also loved.

Burt's Bees: Bring Back the Bees

Burt's Bees can't exist without bees. The fuzzy little bastards are in the name, for crying out loud. Bees are the fundamental center of everything the company produces, and without them, there's no foundation for its products. Supporting those little yellow flying insects is not only an obvious mission for the company, but it's actually critical to the company's future success.

Burt's Bees needs bees to be healthy and thriving. Honestly, humankind needs bees to succeed. Pollination from bees is critical to grow a substantial amount of our food. Burt's Bees recognizes and understands this. If bees are doing well, so are humans. This was the inspiration behind the "Bring Back the Bees" campaign in 2016 and 2017.

Burt's Bees supports hives and gardens on a local level,

but in order to increase its reach, it introduced a limited-edition lip balm, cleverly called Urt's Ees. In conjunction with the new product, it asked followers on Twitter to literally drop the Bs from their tweets and include the hashtag #bringbackthebees. Lea Michele from *Glee* signed on to the campaign as a spokesperson, filming a tutorial video in which she dropped the Bs from her script. At the same time, Burt's Bees dropped the Bs from all of its internal documents, its website, even the URL. For every tweet and every lip balm sold, Burt's Bees planted one thousand wildflowers to provide new bee habitats.

It could not have been a simpler concept, and it ended up as one of Burt's Bees' most successful campaigns. More than 1.5 billion wildflowers were planted in 2016, which is an amazing figure. The campaign drew attention from TV shows, magazines, and other media outlets. But most importantly, Burt's Bees cocreated with its customers in a truly profound way. The brand walked the walk.

Burt's Bees is a true Belief-Driven Brand. While it is always trying to sell its products, it will not compromise on things it doesn't believe in. Even if it's going to hurt the company's bottom line, Burt's Bees won't accept a change that goes against its values and beliefs.

Ponysaurus Brewing

"To alcohol! The cause of, and solution to, all of life's problems." That gem of a quote can be attributed to American TV hero Homer Simpson. Of course, the writers of *The Simpsons* meant it as a humorous line, but it's actually genius. Alcohol—beer, specifically—isn't a fundamentally healthy thing. Like anything, it's best when consumed in moderation.

Beer is fun, and it tastes pretty good, but can it do good? That was the question that Keil Jansen, Nick Johnson, and I sought to answer with the founding of the Ponysaurus Brewing Co., our Durham, North Carolina-based brewery. We didn't want to create a brewery that just existed to give people delicious suds; we wanted our beer to be a force for good by building community.

At the same time, the staff at Baldwin& was looking to create new and unique brands for the agency, but the economic climate at the time worked against some other ideas, which included an app and a chocolate bar. The craft beer scene was exploding in North Carolina, as it was in much of America in the early 2010s. I had been home-brewing beer prior to that, while Keil and Nick had already been in discussions about starting a brewery in the area. A sit-down beer tasting with Keil and Nick, organized by Baldwin& art director Shaun Sundholm, got the wheels spinning, and as they say, the rest is history. It truly was kismet. And in case you're wondering, Keil already had the name Ponysaurus up his sleeve when we started.

I'm fortunate to work for two startups in Baldwin& and Ponysaurus, because the brands' belief systems are built into both business models. We knew from day one with Ponysaurus that we'd wear our values and beliefs on our sleeves for all to see. We had a genuine opportunity to build a different kind of brewery that actually supports causes and builds community. There are breweries out there that do this but not enough; we wanted to be part of that solution.

At a time when North Carolina was in a negative tailspin due to the passage and accompanying fallout of HB2, the highly divisive state-level "bathroom bill" that revoked many antidiscrimination protections from the LGBTQ community, Ponysaurus encouraged people to be more cheerful and tweet more positively. For the 2015 holiday season, we unveiled our "Holiday Spirit Measurer Thingy" in the brewery, online, and in social channels: an interactive, real-time meter that measured the sentiment of people's tweets. With enough "nice" tweets, the tap opened and patrons were treated to our special holiday brew for free. It was a fun idea, created positive action, and helped spread a little cheer.

But getting a bit more serious about HB2, the Ponysaurus Brewing Co. and our Hillsborough, North Carolina, neighbors, Mystery Brewing, knew there was more to be done, so we started an effort to work with other breweries across North Carolina to create a beer to fight back. What was born out of this collaboration was the aptly named beer Don't Be Mean to People, and the response has been extraordinary. The beer has been, and continues to be, sold across the state and in the Ponysaurus brewery itself. All of the profits have gone to LGBTQ causes, including Equality NC, an organization dedicated to equality for the LGBTQ community, and QORDS (Queer Oriented Radical Days of Summer), a summer camp for gay and transgender kids. The brand effort keeps growing and has now spawned our spring "Don't Be Mean to People" Festival, headlined by the band Megafaun with special guests like Sam Beam of Iron & Wine, Tift Merritt, and more. All of the profits from that festival were donated to the American Civil Liberties Union.

Doing this work hasn't been all roses. We've had threats via social media and hateful voice mails, one threatening to burn our brewery down, but that never deterred us. We believe in inclusion and equality. Those are values we hold near and dear. We didn't decide to profit off a controversial situation by just selling beer. In fact, Ponysaurus is actually paying a price to live its values. But guess what?

We're *totally* cool with that. Keil, Nick, and I think there's a future and economic model of success in doing business this way, so we'll keep it up. Are we going to alienate some people? Maybe, but if it's only people who want to burn our brewery to the ground, we're also fine with that. The good news is, we can't make beer fast enough, and we're a valued, engaged part of our community.

Ponysaurus Brewing's identity is built around a nontraditional take on tradition. Everything we try to make is the best version of a traditional thing but in our own unique way. The interior of the brewery is a mix of tradition (pub signs, English pub culture) with a modern ethos, hence our line: "The beer beer would drink if beer could drink beer."

Chipotle

Talk about a brand with a passionate, dedicated fan base. Chipotle has developed a reputation for having *loyal* supporters who will defend it at all costs. Of course, at the end of the day, Chipotle's signature item is a thousand-calorie burrito. No offense to you Chipotle lovers, and I love them, but it isn't exactly the healthiest option out there. You can eat lean and in moderation, of course, but if you're eating its core products every day, you're consuming major calories.

What Chipotle has done is commit to a certain way of

doing business. They've committed to a specific supply chain with specific standards and certifications for their sourcing of ingredients. It might not sound like much, but think of it like a tiny pebble being tossed into a still pond. That initial splash might be a small blip, but the ripples extend farther and farther until they've covered almost the entire pond. That's the type of effect we're talking about. For a fast food company to take a stand like that is game-changing.

Chipotle has hit bumps along the way, particularly with the series of *E. coli* outbreaks in 2015 that garnered significant scrutiny and negative attention, but it hasn't changed the company's approach to doing things the right way.

Warby Parker

If you buy a pair of eyeglasses from Warby Parker, it'll donate a separate pair to someone who needs them. Every time, no questions asked. That commitment is part of the company's business model.

The experience of buying glasses from Warby Parker is as enjoyable as it is user-friendly. You select five pairs of glasses you'd like to try on from their website, and the company then mails trial pairs to you. Once you try them on, you decide whether you want one or all five pairs; it's up to you. However many you want, they'll send to you.

The packaging includes literature that explains the brand's reasoning for donating countless pairs of glasses: everyone has a right to see. It's simple, powerful, and most importantly, genuine. It's done in a non-braggadocious way, too. If you've never ordered from Warby Parker, you probably had no idea they operated this way. Its narrative is a beautiful example of a brand that gives a damn and follows through on its values. The company allows the brand's story to unfold organically as you go through the buying process, which makes it more meaningful.

Toms Shoes

Similar to Warby Parker, Toms Shoes donates a pair of shoes to an impoverished child for every pair sold to its customers. By buying your shoes through Toms Shoes, you know you're having a direct, positive impact on someone else's life. How can you not feel great knowing that?

Toms Shoes also donates a portion of the profits from its recently introduced eyewear sales to help improve eyesight in people in underdeveloped countries. These aren't clever marketing tactics for the mere purpose of selling more products; these are causes that reflect the values and beliefs of the brand. But Tom's Shoes end up selling more products anyway.

Burt's Bees: Intense Hydration

Here's another example from Burt's Bees. To launch its new Intense Hydration line of products in 2012, Burt's Bees needed to drive trial of the product to attract new customers. Trial is hugely important for natural products because there's often skepticism about their effectiveness. Coupon giveaways are certainly not a radically new marketing concept, but the execution of this particular campaign was truly unique. Burt's Bees created a street-level billboard outside of a farmers market in Minneapolis that actually featured two different pictures. The top layer featured a woman's face with wrinkles and fine lines, but it was made up of removable coupons.

As those coupons were removed over the course of the day, it slowly revealed the second picture: a photo of the same woman with healthier, younger-looking skin after eight weeks of using the Intense Hydration products. The billboard was strategically placed in the shadow of Target, one of the biggest distributors of Burt's Bees products, during a major festival at the farmers market. As more and more coupons were peeled off the billboard, the "before" image transitioned into the "after" image, which made for a great time-lapse video for Facebook. We called it the Before and After Coupon Billboard.

The coupon campaign was *wildly* successful. The average redemption rate on coupons is right around 1–3 percent,[33] but the Burt's Bees billboard coupons had a redemption rate of more than 60 percent. It was a multidimensional idea that came together in a great way, but it also featured a second phase. Burt's Bees isn't a company that typically utilizes billboards. Because the company embraces sustainability, the billboard was brought back to North Carolina and converted into a rain catchment system at the Durham School of the Arts. Because it's made out of vinyl, the billboard will last for years in the school's local garden.

By its very nature, advertising is ephemeral. The majority of billboards go up for short periods, come down, and end up in a landfill somewhere. This waste contradicts everything Burt's Bees stands for, so it decided to have its billboard give back to the world through reuse. As we've demonstrated throughout this book, Burt's Bees lives its values and truly walks the walk.

UTEC

The Universidad de Ingeniería y Tecnología (UTEC)

in Lima, Peru, created a billboard in 2013 that collects condensation from the air and converts it into water for residents in a remote village. Anyone from that village could go up to the billboard, turn on a spigot, and pour water into buckets to bring back to their village.

How incredible is that? It's a billboard that literally provides clean water for people who need it. It's still advertising, but it's also converting air into water. That's just amazing. It was the first billboard of its kind, but that's certainly something that can be scaled to help on a larger level. There have been other similar designs, including a billboard with a beehive inside it that dispenses honey.

The key is providing Shared Value while still delivering your message in a way that becomes coveted, appreciated, and useful, rather than annoying and undesirable. This is the brand as a verb, in action. It should live its values and make others aware of those values. That can be accomplished through a billboard, a packaged box, or a website, but simply sharing the narrative of how your brand realized its purpose and values is an ideal way to communicate with customers.

Honey Maid

We've already highlighted Honey Maid and its mission to

support the concept of wholesome, but what *is* "wholesome"? How do you define it, and more importantly, how do you show it? Wholesome food ingredients are only part of the equation.

For Honey Maid, family is wholesome, no matter what shape, size, or color it comes in. In its 2014 "This Is Wholesome" campaign, Honey Maid celebrated all families, including a traditional one with a mother and father, a single-parent version, a nontraditional one with gay parents, and more. They really just showed families being loving families. The thirty-second spots ended with the narrator saying, "Everyday wholesome snacks for every wholesome family."

The response was quite positive and the press attention massive. But Honey Maid was also treated to a smaller barrage of hateful, antigay tweets and mail in response to the commercial, and even though the positive responses outnumbered the negative ones by a ten-to-one margin, it was a sadly predictable outcome. But what Honey Maid did with those responses was beautifully unpredictable. Instead of backing down, Honey Maid printed out the messages and used them to create an art installation forming the word *love*. They literally used hate to create love.

The commercial and the subsequent content showing

the conversion of the hateful responses into a message of unity and love reflected Honey Maid's values. It was smart, it was genuine, and it drew significant engagement from relevant audiences. The art installation also raised money for an organization called Committed to Equality for All. It was a win-win-win.

Ben & Jerry's

Peace, love, and ice cream. That's not just an advertising tagline for Vermont's most famous ice-cream company. Is it catchy? Of course, but is it authentic? Absolutely. They live those values in everything they do as a company. The product is amazing—let's be real, if you're a fan of chunks of delicious things in ice cream, Ben & Jerry's should get the credit as the innovator—but notice the placement of the words in the tagline. The product, "ice cream," comes last after "peace" and "love." Could it be the order is important to them and intended? My guess is, yes, quite intended.

That's because Ben & Jerry's has fully baked (not Half Baked like its wildly popular ice-cream flavor) those two values into the company at the business-model level. Whether it's collaborating with Greyston Bakery, the New York bakery that employs ex-convicts and others from troubled backgrounds, or creating specific ice-cream flavors for specific causes, like Rainforest Crunch, Ben & Jerry's walks the walk.

Ben Cohen, the "Ben" in Ben & Jerry's, helped launch a 2012 grassroots campaign called "Stamp Stampede" in an effort to push for a constitutional amendment to remove money from politics. With small, handheld stamps, people could place short messages on dollar bills in support of the campaign.

In 2016, Ben & Jerry's started another political marketing campaign called "Democracy Is in Your Hands." The accompanying video used nothing but fingers, spoons, and of course, ice cream to explain big money, voting rights, and other political issues. The campaign also included a new ice-cream flavor, cleverly named Empower Mint.

Best of all, this company has fun doing it. Thriving as a Belief-Driven Brand in the Belief Economy shouldn't feel boring or cumbersome. Never take yourself *too* seriously. Ben & Jerry's certainly doesn't.

CHAPTER 7 HIGHLIGHTS

A quick look back at the most salient takeaways from chapter 7:

- **Find the sweet spot:** Baking your core beliefs and values into your brand at a business-model level is how Belief-Driven Brands are defined in the Belief Economy.

- **Examples, examples, examples:** Burt's Bees, Warby Parker, Ben & Jerry's—these are all Belief-Driven Brands thriving in the Belief Economy. The examples contained in this chapter are always worth revisiting.

THE CRIME OF THE CENTURY-ISH: THE GREAT SOCIAL MEDIA HOODWINK.

If you look at the history of social media, it began as an avenue to connect human beings to each other. Facebook, in its infancy, was solely focused on connecting college students on campuses. It might even have truly started out as a new way to meet girls, but I wasn't in that Harvard dorm for its birth. This much I do know: Social media started as a way to create personal engagement with other people, whether it was connecting with your friends, meeting someone new, or reconnecting with old acquaintances.

That might be how social media started, but it has evolved quite a bit in recent years. The minute social media companies become public companies, the focus shifts to the advertising model. Social media platforms are *not* about connecting human beings anymore. They are now an updated version of traditional media channels. Heck, even Facebook Messenger is putting ads into your conversations. "We now interrupt this personal conversation for an important commercial message."

Google, Snapchat, Facebook, and Twitter are major advertising platforms now. They didn't start that way, but that's what they've become. Social media platforms are broadcast networks, albeit with the added dimension of being able to connect with your friends and create a network of conversations and content. For every handful of Facebook posts you scroll past, you'll see some kind of ad. If it's not a generic ad, it might be an AI-generated post that's been tracking your internet behavior for months. Did you look for a new blender online yesterday? Well, here's an ad for them over and over again for the next week. Users have to wade through this wave of advertising on virtually every major social media channel these days.

It's worth noting that the only major platform that hasn't perpetuated the social media lie is LinkedIn (although give it time). It started as a network for connecting professionals and, in my opinion, has remained quite true to that mission so far. It has purchased other companies over the years, but in a strategic way that actively and genuinely supports that goal of connecting professionals across the world.

Social media's evolution from a platform to connect human beings to a platform to advertise to human beings isn't a small change; it's a fundamental switcheroo. We were hoodwinked a bit, to be honest. It would be akin to car companies advertising flying cars, but upon purchasing one, you discover it flies...but only if you're watching commercials the entire time.

There was a time in the early years of social media when companies could have a lowly paid intern running their social channels with no media expenditures. At the time, it was like playing with house money. That free exposure was legitimate, and companies benefited from it. Those days are over.

What It All Means for Brands

Let's face it, Facebook is the eight-hundred-pound gorilla in the room. Social media's transition into the new traditional media of the world was a slow boil, but everything dramatically changed when Facebook went public in 2012. Once Facebook made that move, the company doubled down on an advertising model and never looked back. Facebook used to exist exclusively to connect human beings, but that's no longer the case. For brands, Facebook is now an advertising opportunity. As more social media platforms went public, they all had to generate greater quarterly earnings. How do you do that? Through advertising, of course.

Social media has become the new traditional media.

Don't let this major social media evolution discourage or scare you. Instead, choose to embrace it by reorienting your view of social media. Don't look at it simply as traditional broadcast networks, but instead look at it as a new frontier of broadcast networks. Like the traditional broadcast networks, you'll still have an objective to reach a certain target with your advertising. But unlike the traditional network experience, you'll actually be able to reach those people.

Whereas the old broadcast networks allowed brands to target, say, a specific area code, social media allows brands to target specific people based on similar likes or shared interests. Social media is a really helpful and useful tool, but brands still must always add value to people's lives if they want to connect with them. There are a multitude of ways to define that added value, whether it's something as simple as a funny video, or something more personal such as mixing news with a deal on a new product. It's all about crafting a conversation that not only allows people in but also encourages them to cocreate with your brand and to take action. That's the sweet spot of the Belief Economy.

Take a brand like GoPro, for instance. It doesn't work with an ad agency, but it doesn't need to. All of its customers cocreate advertising with and for it, simply by using the brand's products and posting the content. That is a unique way in which GoPro can connect and collaborate with its customers.

If you're going to do advertising, make it engaging, make it great. Far too many companies still think they can burn their message into people's heads using the techniques of yore instead of actively engaging them. Social media is the most accessible way to engage customers and encourage co-creation.

How to Approach Social Media

Too many companies still view social media as an inexpensive, quick, and opportunistic way to increase their exposure. That's a shortsighted attitude to have. There is absolutely an opportunistic side to social media, where a company can create collaboration as a brand and jump into the conversation with customers, but you can't lose sight of this simple fact: social media has become the new traditional media. Social media platforms are advertising broadcast networks just like traditional TV stations and networks. You *have* to understand that. You can't afford to sweep social media aside and let the unpaid intern handle it on their own.

There's still a prevalent belief that social media content is cheap to create, and in some cases, it's true, like a random viral video of a cat falling into a toilet. Those videos don't take any time or resources to create and have made the notion of what we call "craft" less important in the world of social media than it used to be. That being said, when you do see something crafted in a beautiful and unique way, it often stands out.

Every year, there's a story about a group of college kids who come together and create a commercial for a company like McDonald's that is better than the work being done by its ad agency. And, of course, they do it for free by pulling together friends and getting favors, which is always a compelling part of the narrative. I love those stories, too, but the question becomes, how can those kids make a living doing this kind of work? They can't work for free every time. Having to face this kind of democratized competition from everywhere certainly helps create a very healthy competition and brings out the best in ad agencies by forcing them to adapt to new paradigms. If agencies aren't on top of their game, others will pass them. All of this is to say, we are living in one of the most exciting, albeit challenging, times to be in the advertising business. Almost anything goes.

Eric Shinseki said, "If you dislike change, you're going to hate irrelevance even more."[34] I love that saying, and it's truer than ever in advertising: if you're not constantly changing and evolving, you're not moving forward. Raise your hand if you remember Myspace. Ah, what could have been. Myspace had an amazing platform, but it never changed. It never evolved. It was pretty much asleep at the wheel. Facebook, on the other hand, is constantly adding, subtracting, and tweaking aspects of its user-facing platform. Amazon is the same way. Amazon started as an online bookstore in the 1990s but has since grown exponentially. It never stopped selling books, but it started selling virtually everything else.

What Amazon never did, in contrast to Facebook, was betray its original intended offering. Since 2000, Amazon's logo has been the word *amazon* with an arrow pointing from *a* to *z*. It cleverly forms a smile but also captures the company's essence: they sell everything from A to Z.

Facebook has changed to keep up with the freemium economy. In the freemium economy, brands give away things in order to build their business and then charge customers later by upselling different features or premium benefits. Or they give you something free with the understanding you'll give them something free in return. The screen-sharing service Join.me is a great example of the former. You can join the service for free, but all of the coolest benefits and bonuses are only available to those with paid subscriptions. Google is a great example of the latter. Anyone can open a free Gmail account, but they do so understanding Google will mine and sell their data. Most people don't even consider the price they're paying.

Social Media: Pay to Play?

Facebook, Snapchat, and the other social media platforms are prime opportunities for uniquely customized experiences and co-creation, something near and dear to both millennials and iGen. This is social media's most appealing factor for brands: they can connect you with customers in a personal way like never before. However, if you want to extend your reach and consistently have success, you've got to be prepared to spend money.

Many of the misconceptions about social media are starting to change but not quickly enough. When social media first rose to prominence in the early to mid-2000s, it was seen as the great equalizer because of its organic reach. If your brand ran a video on Facebook, for instance, it could be seen by the majority of the brand's network, no questions asked. But as Facebook continued to change its business model, the algorithms determining who saw posts changed, and organic reach steadily declined. Fast-forward to now, and a brand post that conceivably could have reached upward of 80 percent of the people in its network now reaches only less than 5 percent.

Facebook's change of heart? Pay up, baby. Facebook is a public company fueled by advertising revenue and therefore will always put contingencies in place to make sure brands (large and small) are paying their fair share. When we first launched Ponysaurus, for instance, the majority of those following the brewery's page could see our posts. Those days are over; now we pay to ensure they reach our audience.

To be clear, I don't begrudge Facebook doing this. After all, the ability for brands to reach a platform's audience has never been free. It is well within its right to collect money from brands advertising on its platform. As a marketer, there's no sense in longing for the old days; this is the way it is, and it ain't changing.

Social media is now largely a pay-to-play model, but it's still possible to strike it lucky with something viral. The idea of viral videos, however, is completely misunderstood. Too many companies think they can craft a viral video on command, but the reality is, most of the biggest viral sensations are accidents. Why, for instance, did the ice bucket challenge take the nation by storm during the summer of 2014? It was just a perfect combination of factors: it supported a great cause (curing ALS), it created engagement (by challenging, or gently torturing, your friends), and it was both funny and easy to share. If it was easy to create viral sensations like the ice bucket challenge, why hasn't there been another similar countrywide phenomenon since? More often than not, viral videos are accidents.

Now, it's not *impossible* to engineer something viral. It happens all the time. State Street's "Fierce Girl" statue is a prime example of consciously creating something that resonated with people. It became a hugely viral sensation, almost overnight. So while companies have to earn, and engineer, that type of attention, it's not bad news. In fact, it's very good news; you just have to understand why.

Some brands have a firm grasp on their social media presence, while others are completely clueless. The common thread among most brands, however, is they remain loyal to their own in-house community management team. That's especially true if the person (or people) running their social media accounts are experienced and knowledgeable. Advertising agencies, on the other hand, have to actively seek out those types of relationships, and there's often overlap when social media platforms pitch ideas directly to brands. When Baldwin& was working with Burt's Bees, for example, Twitter would pitch ideas directly to Burt's Bees for social media use. Of course, so would Baldwin&, so ultimately it would come down to Burt's Bees to decide who had best proven out their ideas.

Regardless of which party is overseeing the creation of a brand's social content, we're all battling the same opponent: the Skip button.

Brands versus Skip Button

The concept of the uncanny valley comes from video gaming, but it can be applied to advertising. In video games, the uncanny valley refers to something *too* realistic. The more realistic a developer makes a human's face in a video game, the more noticeably fake it looks to the eye of the person playing the game. It's a fascinating concept, but humans are quite adept at noticing imperfections. Compare extremely real computer animation to something like anime, and you'll see we automatically accept anime without a second thought because it's so unrealistic.

There's an uncanny valley in advertising that occurs as we watch the first few seconds of an ad. When an ad pops up on YouTube, you know almost immediately whether it's a crappy ad worth skipping. If it's the same old annoying ad of someone yelling about something, you'll just start counting the seconds until you can click the Skip button. There are a thousand reasons why we recognize a terrible ad coming at us so fast, but mostly, we're just really good at pattern recognition.

Now, if something unique pops up and catches your attention, you're less likely to hit the Skip button. The series of GEICO "Unskippable" commercials in 2015 are a prime example. The short, fifteen-second YouTube ads featured funny freeze frames in which GEICO "skipped" the commercial for you. They were funny, and they created engagement much higher than the average ad running on YouTube.

What GEICO did so well that many brands overlook is as simple as it is effective: they respected the viewers. People on YouTube want to be entertained, and they want to be engaged. GEICO understands this, and the results were apparent. Here's the truth about the Skip button: the only true way to combat it is to create interesting content people want to watch.

The only true way to combat the Skip button is to create interesting content people want to watch.

As previously stated, everyone says they hate advertising. But it's simply not true; everyone hates *bad* advertising. We all have a favorite commercial or two. People love great advertising. They love to share it, to talk about it, to see it multiple times. These principles are the same, regardless of whether the ad is being viewed on a TV, mobile phone, or computer. Are you engaging someone? Are you giving them the cues there's something worth sticking around for? Are you respecting them as human beings instead of treating them as mindless consumers to be imprinted with your brand's message?

On YouTube, there's an actual Skip button, but every form of advertising is combating its own "Skip button." If an ad doesn't grab a viewer's attention within the first three to five seconds, it'll be tuned out. Many people love the *Breaking Bads* and *Game of Thrones* of the TV landscape, but the reality is, cable series like *NCIS* have better ratings. Series on channels such as CBS, NBC, ABC, and Fox draw more viewers on a consistent basis, so broadcast TV is still a great way to reach a large amount of people. You can get your message out to people through TV and then amplify it through social media, but it's important to remember TV also has a Skip button in the form of fast-forward. The prevalence of DVR keeps the onus on brands to bring their most creative work to the forefront. TV advertising better get its act together or it's doomed, because things are changing fast.

Videri Chocolate Factory

One of Baldwin&'s clients is the Videri Chocolate Factory, a five-year-old chocolate company operating out of Raleigh, North Carolina. I've got to be honest, I love this place so much. Their master chocolate maker is a guy named Sam Ratto, and he's definitely one of the ten most-recognized and -awarded chocolate makers in the country. He's just brilliant, and the chocolate is delicious.

For Videri's fifth anniversary party in January 2017, the company asked Baldwin& to design an invitation. They deeply value connecting with the local community, so naturally they wanted to invite people to the store for free chocolate. They asked for a poster and, maybe, a Facebook post. We took it one step further: we decided to make posters *out of* chocolate. Advertising you can eat.

Sam created the posters himself while we shot a video of him working. The video was then uploaded on Facebook, while the posters were sent to like-minded businesses in high-traffic areas around Raleigh, including DECO Raleigh, a craft store; CAM Raleigh, a contemporary art museum; Whole Foods; and even our lovable little brewery, Ponysaurus. We asked those businesses to post about the chocolate posters on specific days and invite people to come in and eat the posters the next day, all the while sharing the invite for the event on social media. The idea not only helped invite people to Videri's event, but it also increased traffic in the partnering stores and boosted the entire community.

At the end of the day, it was a social media concept, not a chocolate poster idea. The entire idea was in service to giving something simple, in this case chocolate, back to the community, and social media is what made it possible. The entire campaign was unignorably engaging.

güd Social Media

If you couldn't tell by now how much I enjoyed collaborating with Burt's Bees, well, you probably skipped large portions of this book. We've already highlighted a few different collaborative campaigns between Burt's Bees and Baldwin&, but there's one more that registered well on social media.

In 2012, we helped develop a brand called güd under the Burt's Bees umbrella. It was an attempt by Burt's Bees to introduce more millennials to natural products by building their awareness of what was actually in the food they ate, the clothes they wore, and the beauty products they used. There has been a major increase in this awareness in the years since, but back in 2012, it wasn't on a large scale yet.

The güd brand featured products that were 96 percent natural, including lotions and other body creams with intense scents and aromas. Think Bath and Body Works for a comparison. Burt's Bees wanted to create a more natural version of those Bath and Body Works-type products under the güd brand and make it more accessible by selling it for $6.99 at Target.

To encourage co-creation on social media, we designed scratch-and-sniff print ads that doubled as coupons in *Lucky* magazine and *Elle* magazine to reach the target audience of millennial women. Those launch ads featured links to Facebook, so potential customers could scratch and sniff their own coupon while following along on the unique animated video, which followed a woman getting ready for work in the morning. She not only smelled different güd scents on her journey but also interesting smells like rain and wet cement. At the end of the video, if you "liked" the post, you could receive another coupon. It was a fun, unique, and effective way of creating buy-in with millennial women.

The whole idea behind the güd brand was to flip the conventional thought on beauty upside down. Instead of continuing the outdated mindset that if you're beautiful, you'll be happy, güd promoted the idea that if millennial women feel happy, then they feel beautiful. It was a very simple insight but an important one: millennials love to be happy, and they love to show themselves being happy. In fact, the social status update is a new status symbol. We believed every time our customers came into contact with the güd brand, they should smile.

In fact, the social status update is a new status symbol.

After the launch phase, we created a contest on Pinterest called "My Perfect güd Morning." All users had to do to enter was post pictures on Pinterest of their perfect morning with the hashtag #myperfectgudmorning. Once a winner was selected, we "good-napped" her (kidnapping with love and, more importantly, permission), flew her to Africa, and brought her perfect morning board to life. Ten other winners received an item from their Pinterest boards. Again, it's all about co-creation, and the güd brand was built on cocreating with others.

Pinterest is an interesting platform because it offers a utility most other social media platforms don't: you can create your own page to pull together ideas from across the internet. Pinterest isn't at the top of the food chain like Facebook, but it provides a great service.

This book was published at a time when Facebook, You-Tube, Instagram, Twitter, and Snapchat were among the heavyweights in social media. It really wasn't *that* long ago when platforms such as Periscope, Vine, and even Myspace were in the upper echelon. A year or two from now, there will almost certainly be a new social media platform taking the country by storm. This is the ephemeral nature of social media: platforms come and go so fast, and brands have to constantly adapt.

Taco Bell's "Taco Head"

Taco Bell has been one of the leading brands on harnessing the power of social media, particularly Snapchat. In celebration of Cinco de Mayo in 2016, Taco Bell created a fun little Snapchat filter that turned your head into a taco. From there, you could drizzle salsa and other toppings on top to turn yourself into a ready-to-eat taco.

It totally exploded. I'm talking like 200 million views, Super Bowl-type numbers.[35] It was a *smashing* success. You want to talk about establishing co-creation with your customers? With 200 million views, just imagine how many of those people shared their hilarious taco head images with their friends and families.

It might seem simple, but again, simple ideas are often the most powerful ideas. Taco Bell has followed that up with similar filters since, and they are regularly active and engage customers on social media.

CHAPTER 8 HIGHLIGHTS

A quick look back at the most salient takeaways from chapter 8:

- **Social media is the new traditional media:** Platforms such as Facebook and Twitter began as avenues to connect human beings, but they've evolved quite a bit over the years. Social media platforms are the new advertising broadcast networks.

- **Don't skimp on it:** You can't let the unpaid intern handle your brand's social media presence anymore. It's a prime opportunity to create collaboration as a brand and jumpstart the conversation with customers.

- **Be prepared to pay:** The days of organic reach are long gone. Ever since social media companies have gone public, brands have had to pay to ensure they reach their respective audiences.

DO YOU BELIEVE IN THE BELIEF ECONOMY? IT BELIEVES IN YOU.

The influence and decision making of millennials and iGen wielded over the next thirty years will most definitely shape the future of advertising. The world's two youngest generations are coming into power and have given rise to the Belief Economy. Millennials and iGen are less concerned with products themselves than what the brands selling those products stand for.

Brands *must* give a damn, or risk falling into irrelevance. Brands that embrace authentic beliefs and values and strive to have a positive impact on the world will connect with customers in the Belief Economy. Maybe the days of advertisers viewing customers as consumers should come to an end; customers are people and want to be treated as such.

What does this all mean for the future of advertising? Well, it's going to be an uphill battle for advertising agencies as they continue to compete with AI data-collecting bots that see human beings as consumers. This isn't a book about the technological singularity, the hypothetical event in which AI far surpasses humans' intelligence and dramatically changes the world as we know it. But there is a revolution coming, just as there was in the automotive industry with the introduction of assembly lines.

At the same time, more and more advertising agencies are

taking on business consulting work. We're all racing to this fuzzy, undefined middle where everyone is striving to add value, as the big-data AI revolution unfolds simultaneously. Anyone who can definitively say they know what the future holds is probably wrong. When it comes to AI, you can never say never. Technology has given us some of the most incredible advances in society and devices in our personal lives that twenty or thirty years ago we could have never imagined.

It feels like every move you make on the internet is being tracked and used to market to you. We're all constantly being served a product we're interested in, or at least have looked at once before. As overwhelming as the avalanche of messaging feels right now, it has the chance to become unbearable in the future. Who knows? We might even see the introduction of a customer rights bill or similar legislation that prevents 24-7 bombardment.

Part of the problem right now is that AI just isn't smart enough yet. For instance, perhaps my wife asks me to look up the cost of a specific pair of shoes. Well, AI can't differentiate between my wife and me yet, so I will get the follow-up ads on women's shoes. Just to ensure I'm not coming across as a crybaby, it's worth noting that there are ways around this. You can turn certain tracking methods off, and search engines like DuckDuckGo don't track your search history. The genie is out of the bottle, though, and retargeting is here to stay for the foreseeable future. But the real questions that must be answered are: Should I *have* to actively and vigilantly combat internet tracking? Retargeting is an incredibly valuable tool, but are there ways to retarget more responsibly?

What remains unclear about AI is whether it will develop empathy for people. The notion of talking about the impact of a brand on the world is a distinctly human quality. Advertising agencies have the ability to take the Belief Economy into a new territory that, at least for now, AI can't match. This is what advertisers and ad agencies must hold on to, and brands must move beyond relying solely on budgets and numbers.

Brands *must* give a damn, or risk falling into irrelevance.

The Onslaught Industry

We stand on the precipice, staring directly at the oncoming "onslaught industry" of marketing. As an advertiser, you have to decide what you want your role to be within it. Will you say, "Advertising is just there to sell my product, and that's all it should do"? If so, that's your prerogative, but I ask you one simple question: Why? Instead of thinking about your role as advertiser removed from humanity, think about your role as a human, absent advertising.

"But we give a lot of money as a corporation and support fund-raisers. Isn't that enough?" you ask. Of course, that's wonderful and you should keep doing it. Anything to make your community better is fantastic. It's just not what we're talking about unless it ladders up to a bigger point of view for your brand and your company.

Look, I'm a capitalist at heart, so I understand the drive to sell products and meet specific objectives as a marketer. I take it very seriously. It's my job. But I also understand what it's like to be a human being, to love my family, to care deeply about my friends, and to treat others with respect and equality. You're not a mindless consumer of goods; neither are other people. Always remember the new advertising golden rule: Market to people the way you want to be marketed to.

Always remember the new advertising golden rule: Market to people the way you want to be marketed to.

Advertising agencies can stay relevant in the coming years by helping clients to identify the things they give a damn about and to connect through these shared values. There are more tools at advertisers' disposal than ever before, so the positive impact you can create will continue to grow. This is the point that advertising agencies will look back on in years and either say, "Hey, remember when we made some truly positive impact?" or, "Hey, remember when we didn't give a you-know-what about the impact we had?" It's no different than looking back at ads from the 1940s and wondering, "What exactly were they thinking?" By embracing the Belief Economy and your brand's place within it, you can stay ahead of that curve and be part of the solution, not the problem. That's exciting to me as an advertising marketer *and* human being.

How Far We've Come

In the eight-plus years since the founding of our company, there has been a massive enlightenment around the idea of the Belief Economy. When we started in 2009, there was not a lot of talk about generating buy-in through shared values and co-creation. Now we're starting to hear more people talk about it.

The very definition of brand loyalty is changing. No longer is it simply about buying a product; it's about buying into the brand and what it stands for. The traditional selling technique of burning your brand's message into the minds of consumers can give way to a more personal approach in which brands can seek to create buy-in through co-creation, collaboration, and using our work to create Shared Value. What if instead of treating customers as impersonal entities that just purchase products, Belief-Driven Brands treat customers as equals who share a point of view in the world?

I hope I eventually live in a world in which the entire advertising industry operates within the Belief Economy. I truly want the industry to become focused on creating positive impact throughout the world. If that happened, the advertising industry would be unstoppable. If brands created only joy and actionable goodness, people would absolutely love it. They would welcome our messages and activity with open arms, and the age of the Skip button would become irrelevant. When people are delighted and engaged by brands, they won't try to avoid advertising; they'll look for ways to be a part of it, to cocreate through ideas, commercials, videos, advertising campaigns, actions, and behavior.

Advertising is a bad, dirty word these days for some, but the Belief Economy can help change that. Let's create advertising that inspires warm feelings and creates a positive impact and real change.

Your Brand's Next Step

We've covered a lot of information together. Thank you for taking this journey with me, although I expect you're now wondering what your next steps should be. We don't have all the answers, but our guide in the final chapter is designed to get you on your way. It will help steer you in the right direction and ask the pertinent questions that every brand must address as it enters the Belief Economy.

Use the provided tools to create your own positive impact. Be accountable for yourself and your own behavior. In the end, agencies are paid by clients for results but have no final say in the decision-making process. Agencies make recommendations—plenty of them, in fact—but the brands still make the final call.

But remember, it can be pretty damned difficult to objectively view your own environment while you're in it. Or as Howard Gossage is credited as saying, "I don't know who discovered water, but I'm pretty sure it wasn't a fish."

Don't be afraid to reach out for help on this journey. Let's connect and cocreate ourselves. We're in this together, after all.

TOOLS AND EXERCISES

Just to do a very simple recap before we get into a few helpful tools, here's a list of the practices we believe make Belief-Driven Brands irresistible.

What Is a Belief-Driven Brand?

A brand that stands for something beyond the functional benefits of what it makes or does.

The Practices of a Belief-Driven Brand

- Find what you believe in beyond your profit motive
- Talk to people, not consumers
- Understand your why
- Align your brand, products, and company's values with your customers' values and solve their problems
- Don't just reflect a truth; affect a truth
- Your brand is a verb; continually define it by behavior
- Start small if you can't start big, but just start (If you can't start with your business model up, start with your advertising down)
- Always, always, always look for the win-win

A Framework

To tie all of our thinking together, it helps to have a framework. This is a very helpful way to think about the ecosystem of your customers, your brand, and the world they inhabit. It is all connected.

Great marketing has always been rooted in truths. Historically, brands look to uncover an interesting truth and replay it back to the audience in order to create a connection and exhibit empathy and understanding. Belief-Driven Brands don't just uncover and communicate a truth. They change what's true, taking what's currently accepted as the way things are and shaping the world into the way things should be.

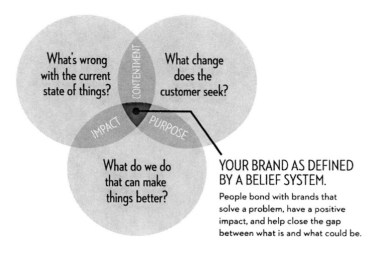

YOUR BRAND AS DEFINED BY A BELIEF SYSTEM.

People bond with brands that solve a problem, have a positive impact, and help close the gap between what is and what could be.

So let's now break this down into actionable steps, and you can either use these tools or create your own. The point is to get on the path.

WHAT'S WRONG WITH THE CURRENT STATE OF THINGS?

Exercise 1

WHAT: Turning "What Is" into "What If"

WHY: Identify what's true about the current state of things in order to create a path forward.

HOW: Using sticky notes, jot down important truths about (1) the customer, (2) the brand, (3) the category, and (4) the culture. Each truth represents the current state of things—the "what is." Then select the most important truths—the ones creating the biggest obstacles for the customer and brand—and begin to brainstorm how to respond to that truth. Each "what is" statement can have a number of different responses. The longer the list, the more potential avenues for giving the brand a bigger role in customers' lives.

Example: A children's apparel company renowned for durable play clothes is losing market share. An examination of "what is" and "what if" can uncover some potential paths forward.

WHAT IS

Children's free time has dropped by twelve hours per week over the past two decades leading to shrinking sales of play clothes.

WHAT IF

- We become advocates for kids and make the case to parents that free time is actually good for their development.
- We make more athletic apparel to fill the growing need of "structured play" apparel.
- We convince moms that although free time is dwindling, competitor brands aren't durable enough to withstand even short, free time sessions.
- And so much more

Exercise 2

WHAT: The Brand Eulogy

WHY: Imagining the absence of the brand can clarify the important role it plays in the world.

HOW: Imagine your brand were to face a sudden and untimely death. Write a eulogy. What were the brand's biggest accomplishments over the course of its life? What was left undone? Remember, it's not just about sales quotas and market share. Focus on the impact the brand has had in the world and could have had had it stuck around a bit longer.

- What relationship did people have with the brand?

  > [blank response box]

- What will the brand be most fondly remembered for?

  > [blank response box]

- How will the world not be the same without it?

  > [blank response box]

Exercise 3

WHAT: Removing the Growth Imperative

WHY: Divorce profit from purpose to help zero in on what makes a brand important.

HOW: If your company didn't have to make money, what would it be doing and who would it be serving? Are there different products or services you might introduce if money were no object? Would you serve different people? Or serve the same people in different ways? Think of how you might take the resources and expertise you have on hand and apply them differently.

....

....

....

....

....

....

WHAT CHANGE DOES THE CUSTOMER SEEK?

Exercise 1

WHAT: Identifying Hopes and Fears

WHY: Distill behaviors down to the most base level (of hopes and fears).

HOW: There are two primary levers that drive human behavior: avoiding negative situations and pursuing positive ones. A target audience is never sitting still. These two dynamics constantly push and pull them in one direction or another. To align with their beliefs, we need to understand not just who they are but also who they want to be. Think about the target audience on three levels: the person (who they are as people), the shopper (how they evaluate options and make decisions), and the user (the experience they have using your product). At each of these levels, list their fears and hopes. Understanding their hopes as a person can be just as important as understanding their hopes for your specific product.

	FEARS	HOPES
THE PERSON		
THE SHOPPER		
THE USER		

Exercise 2

WHAT: Beliefs Lens

WHY: Understand the beliefs that underpin your customers' behaviors.

HOW: In the Belief Economy, it's no longer enough to define a target audience based on who they are (demographics) and what they do (behaviors). To truly connect, we must understand what they believe at their core. By filling out a Beliefs Lens, we can begin to understand what motivates our audience and how we can better align with what they want out of life.

WHAT DO THEY BELIEVE ABOUT...

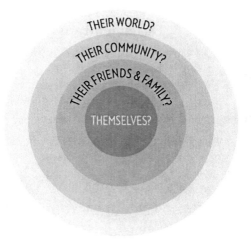

THEIR WORLD?

THEIR COMMUNITY?

THEIR FRIENDS & FAMILY?

THEMSELVES?

Exercise 3

WHAT: Identifying the Sacrifices

WHY: Pinpoint where beliefs and actions are out of alignment.

HOW: Living by your beliefs always requires sacrifice. Where do the customers make sacrifices? Sacrifices are signals as to what beliefs are most important to them. What are they willing to sacrifice? What are they not willing to sacrifice? How might we relieve them of those sacrifices? For this exercise, think about the tensions that exist within the customers' lives. Write them down. Wherever there is a disconnect between what they say they want and what they actually do is fertile territory.

I want to _____**, but it means** _____**.**

EXAMPLES:

I want to be a good provider, **but it means** I have to work long hours, which leaves me less time for my kids.

I want to do what's right for the environment, **but it means** I have to spend more money on energy-efficient light bulbs.

I want to give the contract to an exciting new vendor, **but it means** I might risk my next promotion if things don't work out.

WHAT DO WE DO THAT CAN MAKE THINGS BETTER?

Exercise 1

WHAT: Six-Word Story

WHY: Strip away unnecessary language to get at the essence of your brand.

HOW: It has been said that Ernest Hemingway once wagered his friends that he could craft an entire story in six words. He came up with: "For sale: baby shoes, never worn." In this exercise, force yourself to write a six-word story about your brand. You likely won't nail it on your first attempt, so generate a lot of different options. Forcing yourself to condense the articulation of the brand will help uncover what about the brand is special and unique.

....

Exercise 2

WHAT: The Brand Journey

WHY: Explore the defining moments that shaped the brand's beliefs over time.

HOW: Brands are a culmination of all the actions they took up until this point. While the brand today may not look anything like the brand when it first started, mapping the journey can be enlightening. Create a time line spanning the history of the brand. At its origin, provide details on how the brand was started and why. Fast-forward to where the brand is today, being sure to compare and contrast with the brand in year one. In between those two milestones, mark down the key accomplishments and setbacks along the way. What wars did you win? Which wars did you lose? The journey is likely to have both ups and downs. In hindsight, what would you say is the moral of the story?

Exercise 3

WHAT: Transforming Words into Behavior

WHY: Turn brand descriptors into a set of actions to create impact.

HOW: Traditionally, brands have been a set of perceptions, usually based on specific attributes. A Belief-Driven Brand is about using a set of attributes to create behavior based on a coherent belief system. This in turn helps you determine your impact. Take the list of attributes that are most important to your brand and turn those into verbs. Each of those verbs represents a way your beliefs can manifest themselves out in the world and positively impact the lives of your customers.

EXAMPLE: A brand of breakfast cereal can use the perceptions that already exist about its product and translate them into actions that can help shift it into a Belief-Driven Brand.

DESCRIPTIONS	BEHAVIORS
Wholesome	Providing sustenance
Fun	Creating laughter
Colorful	Brightening mornings
Inclusive	Welcoming everyone
Genuine	Celebrating honesty

Exercise 4

WHAT: Convictions Matrix

WHY: Prioritize which elements of your brand are worth emphasizing.

HOW: Quickly write down all the jobs your brand performs. What does it help people do and accomplish? Once these are written down, begin to score them on a 1–10 scale with 1 being "They don't care at all" to 10 being "They care a lot." How much do customers care about each of the things you do and offer? Which ones do they care about least? Then think about it from the company's perspective. Score each job on another scale of 1–10 with 1 being "We don't enjoy at all" to 10 being "We enjoy a lot." Which jobs do we find most fulfilling? Which ones do we not enjoy as much? Be honest. This exercise is not intended to force you to quit doing certain things but rather to identify where your convictions are strongest.

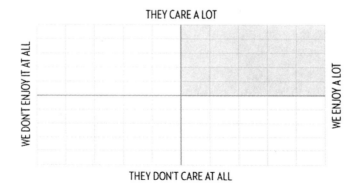

ACKNOWLEDGMENTS

When thinking about writing a book, I always pictured myself holed up in a cabin, fueled by bourbon and a dream, firing off pages at an alarming pace. Alas, this is not how books get written by this author.

It turns out that it takes a village. A village populated by a lot of very smart citizens and one village idiot constantly asking questions and being a general nuisance in the town square.

So thank you to all the people who helped me through this endeavor.

Thank you to my publisher, Elizabeth De Cleyre, who handled me with aplomb and always stayed positive throughout the entire process. And also to Ellie Cole, who made the transition from Elizabeth a very smooth one, as she moved on to a very exciting endeavor involving a certain lifelong dream. Neither of you ever said no to my ever-growing demands for what this might be; in fact, you cheered me on and helped me figure out how to get it done.

Sincere thanks to my editor, Andrew Lovell, who, let's face it, outworked me and kept me sane, organized, and on point, never once complaining about my never-ending emails and last-minute changes, "Last time, I promise." You are an amazing partner on this, and I hope we work together again.

To Katherine Songster, my book developer, who helped me get my structure into shape. I learned a lot about turning a bullet-pointed Word document into a coherent, deeply populated outline.

To all my colleagues at Baldwin&, thank you for your help, your research, your links, your occasional kicks in the pants, and your sincere attempts to not let me make a complete fool of myself. Ashley Yetman, your point of view was a valuable rudder; Sara Carter and Christin Gest, your quick help was invaluable. Erin Bredemann, Jen Hazelett, Bob Ranew, Russell Dodson, David Dykes, Tonya Martin, and Jerry Bodrie, thank you for spending a holiday weekend and more, reading through the manuscript(s), reasoning through the premises put forward, and keeping me on the straight and narrow.

Thanks to Nathan Putens and Kevin Barrett Kane for the badass covers. I dig your businesses and love your work.

Thank you to my sensei, or maybe Jedi Master, Kirk Souder, for helping me see this journey years ago for what it has turned out to be, a life's calling. Your company, Enso, is one monstrously great idea and is setting a high bar for all of us to hit.

Thank you to my friend Dan Carlton, who helped me think

through many things strategic through the years with very informed, formative ideas. His company, the Paragraph Project, has always been a great resource and partner to us for pretty much our entire existence.

Thank you to my friend Jeremy Holden, who is one hell of a smart strategist and someone quite fun to spit truth with over a glass of wine for him and a beer for me. Jeremy's book, *Second That Emotion*, is a great read, people.

To Nick Hawthorne Johnson and Keil Jansen, Rochelle Johnson, and the entire Ponysaurus Brewing crew, thanks for the magical experience and for teaching me every day. I'm so thankful to have you standing shoulder to shoulder with me, believing in what we're up to. "Make no small plans."

To my clients, whom I learn from every day, thank you for being the conveyance for our ideas together and for believing in us. We literally can't do anything without you.

Thanks to Jim Geikie for being the kind of client to always push me to think bigger and for standing steadfastly on your beliefs. You've built a team at Burt's Bees, pound for pound, who can take on anyone in the world, and the list of people is just too big to say everyone's name without leaving someone out.

Thanks to Mike Watson for your trust and constant counsel. You're not only one of the best clients I've ever worked with, you've also taught me about scotch. Talk about a debt.

To Chuck Swoboda, Betty Noonan, and Jackie Woodward, you're not in the book, but in a sense you're all over the book, because you've made me smarter with every interaction.

To Pete Alberse, Brian Berklich, Joe Bowman, Danielle Passingham, thank you for being partners who always keep up the good fight. Kim Garrett, keep having huge ideas.

To Sam Ratto, Starr Sink Ratto, and Chris Heavener for not only being great clients and friends but also for making the best chocolate in the world. In. The. World.

To John Replogle, thank you for the foreword. I'll work my butt off to stay worthy of your kind words. Thank you for setting an example for the rest of us to aspire to; you're truly forging a path others absolutely have to follow, and, man, am I glad you're out there working your magic.

Thanks to Ted Royer for constant late-night counsel and now decades of friendship.

Thanks to Nancy Vonk and Janet Kestin for being role models and coaches and for creating one of the most powerful campaigns in advertising history. No pressure keeping up with you two.

Thanks to the ever-lovely Renee Revaz for not laughing at me when I said I wanted to write a book and for being one hell of a proofreader, thinker, and track-keeper-onner.

And speaking of proofreading/editing, thank you, Amber Saare, for your laser-sharp gaze. I would have probably spelled *laser* with a *z* or something in the previous sentence without you.

Tucker Max, thanks for taking my call.

And finally, thank you to Bill Bernbach, Howard Gossage, Jerry Della Femina, Jim Durfee, Mary Wells, David Ogilvy, and so many more of the giants of our industry. You all showed us that advertising can be something much, much more than someone yelling at you to buy their product.

SOURCES

1. Jeffrey A. Goodby, "The Gossage Galaxy: A Few Words about Howard Luck Gossage, the 'Socrates of San Francisco,' for whom Advertising Was Frequently a Cup of Hemlock," Ad Age, June 1, 1995, http://adage. com/article/news/gossage-galaxy-a-words-howard-luck-gossage-socrates-san-francisco-advertising-frequently-a-cup-hemlock/93841/.

2. Howard Gossage, *Is There Any Hope for Advertising?* (Champaign: University of Illinois Press, 1987), 11.

3. "2017 Edelman Earned Brand," June 18, 2017, https://www.slideshare. net/EdelmanInsights/2017-edelman-earned-brand.

4. "Beyond No Brand's Land," 2017, https://www.edelman.com/earned-brand.

5. George Monbiot, "The Gift of Death," last modified December 10, 2012, http://www.monbiot.com/2012/12/10/the-gift-of-death/.

6. Sebastian Buck, "As Millennials Demand More Meaning, Older Brands Are Not Aging Well," *Fast Company*, October 5, 2017, https://www. fastcompany.com/40477211/as-millennials-demand-more-meaning-older-brands-are-not-aging-well.

7. "Chobani Founder Stands by Hiring Refugees," *CBS News*, last modified April 6, 2017, http://www.cbsnews.com/news/chobani-founder-stands-by-hiring-refugees/.

8. Mary Ellen Shoup, "Chobani Beats Yoplait in Sales and Market Share as Dannon Takes No. 1 Spot in US Yogurt Market," *Dairy Reporter*, last modified March 13, 2017, http://www.dairyreporter.com/ Manufacturers/Chobani-surpasses-Yoplait-in-sales-and-market-share.

9. David M. Bersoff, "The Ideological Shopping Cart," Edelman.com, July 12, 2017, https://www.edelman.com/post/ideological-shopping-cart.

10. Roo Ciambriello, "How Ads That Empower Women Are Boosting Sales and Bettering the Industry," *Adweek*, October 3, 2014, http://www.adweek.com/brand-marketing/how-ads-empower-women-are-boosting-sales-and-bettering-industry-160539/.

11. Jody Holtzman, "What's Your 50+ Strategy? A New Investment Theme," AARP.org, 2013, https://www.aarp.org/content/dam/aarp/home-and-family/personal-technology/2013-09/Longevity-Economy-New-Investment-Theme-AARP.pdf.

12. US Chamber of Commerce Foundation, "The Millennial Generation Research Review," 2012, https://www.uschamberfoundation.org/reports/millennial-generation-research-review.

13. Christopher Donnelly and Renato Scaff, "Who Are the Millennial Shoppers? And What Do They *Really* Want?" Accenture, https://www.accenture.com/us-en/insight-outlook-who-are-millennial-shoppers-what-do-they-really-want-retail.

14. Buck, "As Millennials Demand More Meaning."

15. Wendy D. Manning, "Trends in Cohabitation: Over Twenty Years of Change, 1987–2010," National Center for Family and Marriage Research, http://www.firelands.bgsu.edu/content/dam/BGSU/college-of-arts-and-sciences/NCFMR/documents/FP/FP-13-12.pdf.

16. Alex Williams, "Move Over, Millennials, Here Comes Generation Z," *New York Times*, last modified September 18, 2015, https://www.nytimes.com/2015/09/20/fashion/move-over-millennials-here-comes-generation-z.html.

17. William H. Frey, "Diversity Defines the Millennial Generation," Brookings Institution, last modified June 28, 2016, https://www.brookings.edu/blog/the-avenue/2016/06/28/diversity-defines-the-millennial-generation/.

18. Deep Patel, "Big Brands and Businesses Are Aligning Their Missions with Millennial and Gen Z Consumers," *Forbes*, March 13, 2017, https://www.forbes.com/sites/deeppatel/2017/03/13/big-brands-and-businesses-are-aligning-their-missions-with-millennial-and-gen-z-consumers/#56de133f5a41.

19. Erik Samdahl, "New i4cp Research: 93% of Gen Z Says Societal Impact Affects Where They Work," i4cp, December 16, 2015, https://www.i4cp.com/productivity-blog/2015/12/16/new-i4cp-research-93-of-gen-z-says-societal-impact-affects-where-they-work.

20. Verena Dobnik, "'Fearless Girl' Statue Stares Down Wall Street's Iconic Bull," Associated Press, last modified March 8, 2017, http://boston.cbslocal.com/2017/03/08/girl-statue-wall-street-bull-international-womens-day/.

21. Bourree Lam, "Why People Are So Upset about Wall Street's 'Fearless Girl,'" *The Atlantic*, last modified April 24, 2017, https://www.theatlantic.com/business/archive/2017/04/fearless-girl-reactions/523026/.

22. Michael E. Porter and Mark R. Kramer, "Creating Shared Value," *Harvard Business Review*, last modified January 2017, http://www.creativeinnovationglobal.com.au/wp-content/uploads/Shared-value-Harvard-business-review.pdf.

23. Maureen Morrison, "Papa John's Faces Backlash in Wake of Obamacare Comments," Ad Age, last modified November 14, 2012, http://adage.com/article/news/papa-john-s-faces-backlash-wake-obamacare-comments/238316/.

24. Antonio Vives, "When Creating Shared Value Causes Value Destruction: The Case of Nespresso," Triple Pundit, last modified April 28, 2016, http://www.triplepundit.com/2016/04/when-creating-shared-value-can-lead-to-value-destruction-the-case-of-nespresso/.

25. Rosemary Feitelberg, "New Survey Ranks Nike First for Brand Intimacy with Consumers, Followed by Levi's, Under Armour," WWD, July 6, 2016, http://wwd.com/fashion-news/fashion-scoops/nike-brand-loyalty-consumers-followed-by-levis-under-armour-10482190/.

26. Al Ries and Jack Trout, "The Positioning Era Cometh," AdAge, http://www.ries.com/positioning-era/.

27. Emma Hall, "IPA Report: Ads that Win Awards Are 11 Times More Effective," Ad Age, last modified July 14, 2010, http://adage.com/article/global-news/ipa-report-ads-win-awards-11-times-effective/144942/.

28. Heather Clancy, "Walmart Commits to Massive LED Lighting Rollout," *Forbes*, last modified April 9, 2014, https://www.forbes.com/sites/heatherclancy/2014/04/09/walmart-commits-to-massive-led-lighting-rollout/#37a114d51eef.

29. "Big Beef Buyers," *Beef Magazine*, last modified February 1, 2007, http://www.beefmagazine.com/mag/beef_big_beef_buyers.

30. Loren Grush, "How Bad Is Soda, Really?" *Prevention*, last modified August 17, 2013, http://www.prevention.com/food/healthy-eating-tips/how-bad-soda-really.

31. E. J. Schultz and Ann-Christine Diaz, "Pepsi Is Pulling Its Widely Mocked Kendall Jenner Ad," Ad Age, last modified April 5, 2017, http://adage.com/article/cmo-strategy/pepsi-pulling-widely-mocked-kendall-jenner-ad/308575/.

32. Sara Spary, "Unilever: Brands that Stand for Something Grow Twice as Fast," *Campaign*, last modified October 6, 2015, http://www.campaignlive.co.uk/article/unilever-brands-stand-something-grow-twice-fast/1367224#Y1QoAS87orwo8E4i.99.

33. Brandon Carter, "Coupon Statistics: The Ultimate Collection," Access, last modified May 23, 2017, http://blog.accessdevelopment.com/ultimate-collection-coupon-statistics.

34. "Eric Shineski," *Wikipedia*, last modified March 20, 2016, https://en.wikiquote.org/wiki/Eric_Shinseki.

35. Lauren Johnson, "Taco Bell's Cinco de Mayo Snapchat Lens Was Viewed 224 Million Times," *Adweek*, last modified May 11, 2016, http://www.adweek.com/digital/taco-bells-cinco-de-mayo-snapchat-lens-was-viewed-224-million-times-171390/.

DAVID BALDWIN

One of the most honored figures in the advertising industry, **DAVID BALDWIN** is the founder of Baldwin&, which was named Ad Age's Small Agency of the Year, twice named Ad Age's Campaign of the Year, and also named the 4A's Creative Small Agency of the Year. He is the former chairman of The One Club in New York City and served as executive producer on *Art & Copy* and associate producer on *The Loving Story*, two Emmy Award-winning films. His advertising work has been recognized by *The One Show*, Cannes, D&AD, the Clio Awards, and other institutions and organizations. David is also the cofounder and brand master of the Ponysaurus Brewing Co. and a former guitarist/songwriter for the band Pants!

CPSIA information can be obtained
at www.ICGtesting.com
Printed in the USA
LVOW09*1607250418
573731LV00001BA/3/P